D0229074

Powys

37218 00432009 4

STEP-BY-STEP
cakes

STEP-BY-STEP

cakes

Caroline Bretherton

LONDON, NEW YORK,
MUNICH, MELBOURNE, DELHI

Editorial Assistant David Fentiman
Senior Editor Alastair Laing
Project Art Editor Kathryn Wilding
Senior Art Editor Sara Robin
Managing Editor Dawn Henderson
Managing Art Editor Christine Keilty
Senior Jacket Creative Nicola Powling
Production Editor Siu Chan
Production Controller Claire Pearson
Creative Technical Support Sonia Charbonnier
Photographers Howard Shooter, Michael Hart

DK INDIA
Assistant Editor Ekta Sharma
Designer Prashant Kumar
Managing Editor Glenda Fernandes
Managing Art Editor Navidita Thapa
DTP Manager Sunil Sharma
DTP Operator Rajdeep Singh

First published in Great Britain in 2012
by Dorling Kindersley Limited
80 Strand, London WC2R 0RL

Penguin Group (UK)

2 4 6 8 10 9 7 5 3 1
001 – 180675 – May/2012

Copyright © 2012 Dorling Kindersley Limited

All rights reserved. No part of this publication
may be reproduced, stored in a retrieval system,
or transmitted in any form or by any means,
electronic, mechanical, photocopying, recording,
or otherwise without the prior written permission
of the copyright owners.

A CIP catalogue record for this book
is available from the British Library

ISBN 978-1-4053-6824-7

Colour reproduction by
Media Development Printing Ltd, UK

Printed and bound in Singapore by Tien Wah Press

Discover more at www.dk.com

Contents

Chocoholic

Triple-Layer Chocolate Cake
page 42

15 MINS | 30–35 MINS

Chocolate and Hazelnut Brownies page 182

25 MINS | 12–15 MINS

Chocolate and Brazil Nut Cake page 38

25 MINS | 45–50 MINS

Prune Chocolate Dessert Cake page 70

30 MINS | 40–45 MINS

Chocolate Cake
page 40

30 MINS | 20–25 MINS

Black Forest Gâteau
page 80

55 MINS | 40 MINS

Pear and Chocolate Cake
page 43

15 MINS | 30 MINS

Sour Cherry and Chocolate Brownies page 186

15 MINS | 20–25 MINS

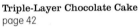

Chocolate Fudge Cake
page 46

Baked Chocolate Mousse
page 48

40 MINS   30 MINS

20 MINS   1 HOUR

Chocolate Chestnut Roulade
page 76

Chocolate Cupcakes
page 100

50-55 MINS   5-7 MINS

20 MINS   20-25 MINS

Chocolate Amaretti Roulade
page 78

25-30 MINS   20 MINS

Chocolate Fudge Cake Balls
page 104

35 MINS   25 MINS

Chocolate Fondants
page 114

20 MINS   5-15 MINS

Chocolate Millefeuilles
page 92

2 HOURS   25-30 MINS

Get Fruity

**Blueberry Upside Down
Cake** page 56

15 MINS　40 MINS

Cherry and Almond Cake
page 57

20 MINS　1½–1¾ HOURS

Cherry Flapjacks
page 180

15 MINS　25 MINS

Rich Fruit Cake
page 66

25 MINS　2½ HOURS

Light Fruit Cake
page 71

25 MINS　1¾ HOURS

Plum Pudding
page 72

45 MINS　8–10 HOURS

Angel Food Cake
page 20

30 MINS　35–45 MINS

**Génoise Cake with Raspberries
and Cream** page 22

30 MINS　25–30 MINS

Lemon Polenta Cake
page 36

30 MINS　50–60 MINS

Lemon and Blueberry Muffins
page 116

20–25 MINS 15–20 MINS

German Apple Cake
page 50

30 MINS 45–50 MINS

Bavarian Plum Cake
page 58

35–40 MINS 50–55 MINS

Banana Bread
page 60

20–25 MINS 35–40 MINS

Raspberry Cream Meringues
page 134

10 MINS 1 HOUR

Strawberries and Cream Macarons page 158

30 MINS 18–20 MINS

Strawberry Shortcakes
page 125

15–20 MINS 12–15 MINS

Summer Fruit Millefeuilles
page 93

2 HOURS 25–30 MINS

Great for Kids

RECIPE CHOOSERS

Vanilla Cream Cupcakes
page 96

20 MINS | 20–25 MINS

Fondant Fancies
page 102

20–25 MINS | 25 MINS

Gingerbread Men
page 148

20 MINS | 10–12 MINS

Whoopie Pies
page 108

40 MINS | 12 MINS

Strawberries and Cream Whoopie Pies page 113

40 MINS | 12 MINS

Apple Muffins
page 119

10 MINS | 20–25 MINS

Hazelnut and Raisin Oat Cookies page 140

20 MINS | 10–15 MINS

White Chocolate and Macadamia Nut Cookies page 143

25 MINS | 10–15 MINS

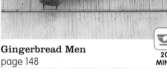

Spiced Carrot Cake
page 33

20 MINS | 30 MINS

Chocolate Cupcakes
page 100

20 MINS | 20–25 MINS

Fast and Fabulous

Madeleines
page 120

15–20 MINS · 10 MINS

Welsh Cakes
page 126

20 MINS · 16–24 MINS

Swedish Spice Biscuits
page 150

20 MINS · 10 MINS

Canestrelli
page 152

20 MINS · 15–20 MINS

Swiss Roll
page 24

20 MINS · 12–15 MINS

Pistachio and Cranberry Oat Cookies page 142

20 MINS · 10–15 MINS

Macaroons
page 154

10 MINS · 12–15 MINS

Cinnamon Stars
page 151

20 MINS · 12–15 MINS

Chocolate Fondants
page 114

20 MINS · 5–15 MINS

Chocolate Muffins
page 118

10 MINS · 15 MINS

everyday cakes

Victoria Sponge Cake

Probably the most iconic British cake, a good Victoria sponge should be well-risen, moist, and light.

SERVES 6–8 | **30 MINS** | **20–25 MINS** | **4 WEEKS, UNFILLED**

Special equipment
2 x 18cm (7in) round cake tins

Ingredients
175g (6oz) unsalted butter, softened, plus extra for greasing
175g (6oz) caster sugar
3 eggs
1 tsp vanilla extract
175g (6oz) self-raising flour
1 tsp baking powder

For the filling
50g (1¾oz) unsalted butter, softened
100g (3½oz) icing sugar, plus extra to serve
1 tsp vanilla extract
115g (4oz) good-quality seedless raspberry jam

1 Preheat the oven to 180°C (350°F/Gas 4). Grease the tins and line with parchment.

2 Whisk the butter and sugar in a bowl for 2 minutes, or until pale, light, and fluffy.

3 Add the eggs one at a time, mixing well between additions to avoid curdling.

4 Add the vanilla extract and whisk briefly until it is well-blended through the batter.

5 Whisk the mixture for another 2 minutes until bubbles appear on the surface.

6 Remove the whisk, then sift the flour and baking powder into the bowl.

7 With a metal spoon, gently fold in the flour until just smooth; try to keep the mixture light.

8 Divide the mixture evenly between the tins and smooth the tops with a palette knife.

9 Cook for 20–25 minutes or until golden brown and springy to the touch.

10 Test the sponges by inserting a skewer. If it comes out clean, the cakes are cooked.

11 Leave for a few minutes in the tins. Turn out, good side up, onto a wire·rack to cool.

12 For the filling, beat together the butter, icing sugar, and vanilla extract until smooth.

13 Spread the buttercream evenly onto the flat side of a cooled sponge with a palette knife.

14 Gently spread the jam on top of the buttercream using a table knife.

15 Top with the second sponge, flat sides together. Serve dusted with sifted icing sugar.

STORE The filled cake will keep in an airtight container in a cool place for 2 days.
PREPARE AHEAD Unfilled, the sponges will keep for up to 3 days.

Victoria Sponge Cake variations

Coffee and Walnut Cake

A slice of coffee and walnut cake is the perfect accompaniment to morning coffee. Here the cake is made in smaller tins than the classic Victoria sponge to give it extra height and impact.

SERVES 8	20 MINS	20–25 MINS	8 WEEKS, UNFILLED

Special equipment
2 x 17cm (6¾in) round cake tins

Ingredients
175g (6oz) unsalted butter, softened, plus extra for greasing
175g (6oz) soft light brown sugar
3 eggs
1 tsp vanilla extract
175g (6oz) self-raising flour
1 tsp baking powder
1 tbsp strong coffee powder, mixed with 2 tbsp boiling water and cooled

For the icing
100g (3½oz) unsalted butter, softened
200g (7oz) icing sugar
9 walnut halves

Method

1 Preheat the oven to 180°C (350°F/Gas 4). Grease the tins and line the bases with parchment. Cream together the butter and sugar in a bowl, using an electric whisk, until light and fluffy.

2 Add the eggs one at a time, beating well between additions. Add the vanilla, and whisk for 2 minutes until bubbles appear on the surface. Sift in the flour and baking powder.

3 Gently fold in the flour, followed by half the coffee mixture. Divide the batter evenly between the prepared tins, and smooth the tops with a palette knife.

4 Cook for 20–25 minutes or until golden brown and springy to the touch. Test by inserting a skewer; if it comes out clean, the cakes are cooked. Leave for a few minutes, then turn out onto a wire rack to cool.

5 To make the filling, beat the butter and icing sugar together until smooth. Beat in the remaining coffee mixture. Spread half the buttercream evenly onto the flat side of one of the cakes. Top with the second cake, flat sides together, and spread with the remaining buttercream. Decorate with the walnut halves.

STORE The cake will keep in an airtight container in a cool place for 3 days.

Madeira Cake

In this simple cake the flavours of lemon and butter shine through.

SERVES 8–10	20 MINS	50–60 MINS	UP TO 8 WEEKS

Special equipment
18cm (7in) round springform cake tin

Ingredients
175g (6oz) unsalted butter, softened, plus extra for greasing
175g (6oz) caster sugar
3 eggs
225g (8oz) self-raising flour
finely grated zest of 1 lemon

Method

1 Preheat the oven to 180°C (350°F/Gas 4). Butter the cake tin and line the base and sides with baking parchment.

2 Cream the butter and sugar with an electric whisk for about 2 minutes, until light and fluffy. Add the eggs one at a time, mixing well between additions.

3 Whisk for 2 minutes until bubbles appear on the surface. Sift in the flour and add the lemon zest. Gently fold in the flour and zest until just smooth.

4 Spoon the mixture into the tin. Bake for 50 minutes–1 hour or until a skewer comes out clean. Leave the cake in the tin for a couple of minutes, then turn out onto a wire rack to cool. Remove the parchment.

STORE The cake will keep in an airtight container for 3 days.

BAKER'S TIP
The secret to a good, light Victoria sponge-style cake is to ensure that as little air as possible is lost during the folding-in stage, when the flour is added. For an even lighter finish, use baking margarine; the higher water content seems to bake air into the cake, though butter gives a richer flavour.

Marble Loaf Cake

For a twist on a classic sponge mixture, divide the batter in two and flavour half with cocoa before mixing them together for a wonderful marbled effect.

SERVES 8–10	25 MINS	45–50 MINS	UP TO 8 WEEKS

Special equipment
900g (2lb) loaf tin

Ingredients
175g (6oz) unsalted butter, softened, plus extra for greasing
175g (6oz) caster sugar
3 eggs
1 tsp vanilla extract
150g (5½oz) self-raising flour
1 tsp baking powder
25g (scant 1oz) cocoa powder

Method

1 Preheat the oven to 180°C (350°F/Gas 4). Grease the loaf tin and line the base with baking parchment.

2 Using an electric whisk on medium speed, cream together the butter and sugar for about 2 minutes, until light and fluffy. Add the eggs one at a time, beating well between additions. Add the vanilla extract, and whisk for another 2 minutes until bubbles appear on the surface. Sift in the flour and baking powder.

3 Divide the batter evenly between 2 bowls. Sift the cocoa powder into 1 bowl and gently fold in. Pour the vanilla cake batter into the loaf tin, then top with the chocolate batter. Using the end of a wooden spoon, a knife, or a skewer, swirl the 2 mixtures together, creating a marbled effect.

4 Bake for 45–50 minutes or until a skewer comes out clean. Leave to cool slightly, then turn out onto a wire rack. Remove the baking parchment.

STORE The cake will keep in an airtight container for 3 days.

Angel Food Cake

This American classic is named for its almost pure white sponge that is as light as air. Fat-free, it does not keep well and is best eaten the same day.

| SERVES 8–12 | 30 MINS | 35–45 MINS |

Special equipment
1.7-litre (3-pint) ring mould
sugar thermometer

Ingredients
large knob of butter, for greasing
150g (5½oz) plain flour
100g (3½oz) icing sugar

8 egg whites
  (keep the yolks for custards and tart fillings)
pinch of cream of tartar
250g (9oz) caster sugar
few drops of almond or vanilla extract

For the frosting
150g (5½oz) caster sugar
2 egg whites
strawberries (halved), blueberries,
  and raspberries, to decorate
icing sugar, for dusting

Method

1 Preheat the oven to 180°C (350°F/Gas 4). Melt the butter in small pan and use to generously brush the inside of the ring mould. Sift the flour and icing sugar into a bowl (see Baker's Tip).

2 Whisk the egg whites and cream of tartar until stiff, then whisk in the caster sugar, 1 tablespoon at a time. Sift in the flour mixture and gradually fold it in with a metal spoon, then fold in the almond or vanilla extract.

3 Spoon the mixture gently into the ring mould, filling right to the brim, and level the surface with a palette knife. Place the mould on a baking tray and bake for 35–45 minutes or until just firm to the touch.

4 Carefully remove the cake from the oven, and invert the mould onto a wire rack. Leave the cake to cool, then ease it out of the mould.

5 To make the frosting, place the caster sugar in a saucepan with 4 tablespoons of water. Heat gently, stirring, until the sugar dissolves. Boil until the syrup reaches a soft-ball stage (114–118°C/238–245°F), or until a little of the syrup forms a soft ball when dropped into very cold water.

6 Meanwhile, whisk the egg whites until stiff. As soon as the sugar syrup reaches the correct temperature, plunge the base of the pan into cold water to stop the syrup getting any hotter. Pour the sugar syrup into the egg whites while whisking, pouring in a slow, steady stream into the centre of the bowl. Keep whisking for about 5 minutes, until stiff peaks form.

7 Working quickly, because the frosting will set, spread it thinly all over the inside and outside of the cake with a palette knife, swirling the surface to create texture. Top with strawberries, blueberries, and raspberries, and dust over icing sugar using a fine sieve.

BAKER'S TIP

Sifting the flour twice produces a very light cake. For best results, try to lift the sieve high above the bowl, allowing the flour to come into contact with as much air as possible as it floats down. For an even lighter cake, sift the flour twice before sifting again into the egg mixture.

Génoise Cake with Raspberries and Cream

This delicate, whisked sponge makes an impressive dessert, but is also perfect as the centrepiece for an afternoon tea on a sunny summer's day.

SERVES 8–10	30 MINS	25–30 MINS	4 WEEKS, UNFILLED

Special equipment
20cm (8in) round springform cake tin

Ingredients
40g (1½oz) unsalted butter,
  plus extra for greasing
4 large eggs
125g (4½oz) caster sugar
125g (4½oz) plain flour
1 tsp vanilla extract
finely grated zest of 1 lemon
75g (2½oz) raspberries, to decorate (optional)

For the filling
450ml (15fl oz) double or whipping cream
325g (11oz) raspberries
1 tbsp icing sugar, plus extra for dusting

Method

1 Melt the butter and reserve. Preheat the oven to 180°C (350°F/Gas 4). Grease the cake tin and line the base with parchment.

2 Bring a pan of water to the boil, remove from the heat and stand a heatproof bowl over the top. Add the eggs and sugar and whisk, using an electric whisk, for 5 minutes until the whisk leaves a trail when lifted; the mixture will expand up to 5 times its original volume. Remove the bowl from the pan and whisk for another minute to cool.

3 Sift in the flour and carefully fold it into the mixture. Fold in the vanilla, lemon zest, and melted butter.

4 Put the mixture into the tin and bake for 25–30 minutes or until the top is springy and light golden brown. A skewer inserted into the middle of the cake should come out clean.

5 Leave the cake to cool in its tin for a few minutes, then turn out onto a wire rack and cool completely. Remove the parchment.

6 When the cake is cold, carefully cut it horizontally into three equal pieces, using a serrated bread knife.

7 In a large bowl, whip the cream until stiff. Lightly crush the raspberries with the icing sugar and fold into the cream, leaving behind any juice so that the cream is not too wet.

8 Place the bottom slice of cake on a serving plate and spread with half the cream mixture. Top with the second slice, spread with the remaining cream, and then place the final slice on top. Decorate with raspberries, if using, and dust the cake with icing sugar. Serve immediately.

PREPARE AHEAD The sponge will keep in an airtight container for 1 day before being cut and filled.

BAKER'S TIP
This is a classic Italian cake that uses only a little melted butter for flavouring. These cakes are infinitely adaptable, and can be filled with anything you like, but should ideally be eaten within 24 hours of baking, since the lack of fat means they do not store as well as other cakes.

EVERYDAY CAKES

Swiss Roll

There is a trick to rolling up a Swiss roll – follow these simple steps and yours will come out perfectly.

SERVES 8–10	20 MINS	12–15 MINS	UP TO 8 WEEKS

Special equipment
32.5 x 23cm (13 x 9in) Swiss roll tin

Ingredients
3 large eggs
100g (3½oz) caster sugar, plus extra for sprinkling
pinch of salt
75g (2½oz) self-raising flour
1 tsp vanilla extract
6 tbsp raspberry jam (or use any other type of jam, or chocolate-hazelnut spread), for the filling

EVERYDAY CAKES

1 Preheat the oven to 200°C (400°F/Gas 6). Line the base of the tin with baking parchment.

2 Set a bowl over a pan of simmering water; the base of the bowl shouldn't touch the water.

3 Add the eggs, sugar, and salt and whisk with an electric whisk for 5 minutes until thick.

4 Test the egg mixture: drips from the beaters should sit on the surface for a few seconds.

5 Remove the bowl from the pan, place it on a work surface. Whisk for 1–2 minutes until cool.

6 Sift in the flour, add the vanilla extract, and gently fold in, trying to keep the volume.

7 Pour into the tin and gently level into all the corners, smoothing the top with a palette knife.

8 Bake for 12–15 minutes in the preheated oven until firm and springy to the touch.

9 Check the cake has shrunk away slightly from the sides of the tin; this shows it is ready.

10 Sprinkle a sheet of baking parchment evenly with a thin layer of caster sugar.

11 Carefully turn the Swiss roll out of its tin onto the caster sugar, so it lies upside down.

12 Leave to cool for 5 minutes, then carefully peel the baking parchment from the cake.

13 For the filling, if the jam is too thick to spread, warm it gently in a small pan.

14 Spread the jam over the top of the cake, spreading to the edge with a palette knife.

15 Make an indent with the back of a knife along one short side, 2cm (¾in) from the edge.

16 Using the indented edge to start it off, gently but firmly roll it up, using the parchment.

17 Use the baking parchment to keep the cake tightly rolled and in shape. Leave to cool.

18 When ready to serve, unwrap the cake and place it, join downwards, on a serving plate. Sprinkle with extra caster sugar. **STORE** The roll will keep in an airtight container for 2 days.

Swiss Roll variations

Orange and Pistachio Swiss Roll

Using the delicate flavours of pistachio nuts and orange flower water gives this classic recipe a slightly more modern twist. It is easily portioned and makes an ideal dessert for large parties and buffets.

SERVES 8	20 MINS	15 MINS	8 WEEKS UNFILLED

Special equipment
32.5 x 23cm (13 x 9in) Swiss roll tin

Ingredients
3 large eggs
100g (3½oz) caster sugar, plus extra for sprinkling
pinch of salt
75g (2½oz) self-raising flour
finely grated zest of 2 oranges, and 3 tbsp juice
2 tsp orange flower water (optional)
200ml (7fl oz) double cream
75g (2½oz) unsalted pistachio nuts, chopped
icing sugar, for dusting

Method
1 Preheat the oven to 200°C (400°F/Gas 6). Line the tin with baking parchment. Set a bowl over a pan of simmering water. Whisk the eggs, sugar, and salt with an electric whisk for 5 minutes until thick and creamy.

2 Remove the bowl from the pan and whisk for another 1–2 minutes until cool. Sift in the flour, add half the orange zest, and 1 tablespoon of juice. Gently fold together. Pour into the tin and bake for 12–15 minutes until firm to the touch.

3 Sprinkle a sheet of baking parchment with caster sugar. Turn out the cake onto the sugar. Leave to cool for 5 minutes, then peel off the parchment from the cake and discard. Sprinkle with the orange flower water (if using).

4 Make an indent with the back of a knife along one short side, about 2cm (¾in) from the edge. Using the indent to start it off, roll up the cake around the sugared parchment (see Baker's Tip). Leave to cool.

5 Whip the cream and fold in the pistachios, the remaining orange zest, and juice. Unroll the cake, discard the parchment, and spread the cream filling evenly over the surface. Roll up the cake again and place join downwards on a serving plate. Dust with icing sugar just before serving.

ALSO TRY...
Lemon Swiss Roll Instead of orange, fold in lemon zest and juice to the cake mix, then fill with 300g (10oz) lemon curd.

> **BAKER'S TIP**
> If a recipe requires a Swiss roll to be completely cool before filling, the cake will need to be rolled into shape while still warm, and then unrolled. Roll the cake around a fresh sheet of parchment paper. This will prevent the layers from sticking and allow the cake to be rolled tightly for a neat shape, and easily unrolled.

Spanish Rolled Sponge Cake

In this sophisticated Spanish take on Swiss roll, a tangy lemon sponge is rolled around a smooth filling of chocolate-rum ganache, forming a pretty spiral for slicing. Impressive as a dinner party dessert. ▶

SERVES 8–10	40–45 MINS	7–9 MINS	8 WEEKS, UNFILLED

Chilling time
6 hours

Ingredients
butter, for greasing
150g (5½oz) caster sugar
5 eggs, separated
finely grated zest of 2 lemons
45g (1½oz) plain flour, sifted
pinch of salt
125g (4½oz) dark chocolate, coarsely chopped
175ml (6fl oz) double cream
1½ tsp ground cinnamon
1½ tbsp dark rum
60g (2oz) icing sugar
candied lemon zest, to serve (optional)

Method
1 Preheat the oven to 220°C (425°F/Gas 7). Grease and line a baking sheet with parchment. Mix 100g (3½oz) caster sugar with the egg yolks and zest. With an electric whisk, beat for 3–5 minutes until thick. In a separate bowl, whisk the egg whites until stiff. Add the remaining sugar and whisk until glossy. Add salt to the yolk mix, then sift and fold in the flour, and the egg whites.

2 Pour the mixture onto the baking sheet and spread it almost to the edges. Bake near the bottom of the oven for 7–9 minutes until firm and golden brown.

3 Turn out onto another baking sheet and remove the parchment. Make an indent with the back of a knife along one short side, 2cm (¾in) from the edge. Using the indent to start it off, tightly roll the cake up around a piece of parchment (see Baker's Tip). Leave to cool.

4 For the ganache, put the chocolate in a large bowl. Heat the cream with ½ teaspoon of cinnamon in a saucepan until almost boiling. Add to the chocolate and stir until melted. Let cool and add the rum. Beat the ganache with an electric whisk for 5–10 minutes until thick and fluffy.

5 Mix half the icing sugar with 1 teaspoon cinnamon and evenly sieve over a sheet of parchment. Unroll the cake onto the sugared paper. Spread the ganache, then carefully roll up and wrap with parchment. Chill for 6 hours until firm. Unwrap the cake, trim each end, sift over the remaining icing sugar and scatter with candied lemon zest (if using).

Ginger Cake

Deeply flavoured with preserved ginger, this rich and moist ginger cake is a firm favourite, and keeps well for up to a week – should it last that long!

| SERVES 12 | 20 MINS | 35–45 MINS | UP TO 8 WEEKS |

Special equipment
18cm (7in) square cake tin

Ingredients
110g (4oz) unsalted butter, softened, plus extra for greasing
225g (8oz) golden syrup
110g (4oz) soft dark brown sugar
200ml (7fl oz) milk

4 tbsp syrup from preserved ginger jar
finely grated zest of 1 orange
225g (8oz) self-raising flour
1 tsp bicarbonate of soda
1 tsp mixed spice
1 tsp cinnamon
2 tsp ground ginger
4 pieces of preserved stem ginger, finely chopped and tossed in 1 tbsp plain flour
1 egg, lightly beaten

Method

1 Preheat the oven to 170°C (340°F/Gas 3½). Grease the cake tin and line the base with baking parchment.

2 In a saucepan, gently heat the butter, golden syrup, sugar, milk, and ginger syrup until the butter has melted. Add the orange zest and leave to cool for 5 minutes.

3 In a large mixing bowl, sift together the flour, bicarbonate of soda, and ground spices. Pour the warm syrup mixture into the dry ingredients and beat them well, using a balloon whisk. Stir in the preserved ginger and egg.

4 Pour the batter into the tin and cook for 35–45 minutes until a skewer inserted into the middle of the cake comes out clean. Leave to cool in the tin for at least 1 hour before turning out onto a wire rack. Remove the baking parchment before serving.

STORE This cake is very moist and keeps well in an airtight container for up to 1 week.

BAKER'S TIP
The use of golden syrup and dark brown sugar here gives a dense, moist cake that keeps very well. If the cake is beginning to get a little dry with age, try slicing it and spreading with butter as a breakfast snack, or even turning it into a rich version of the Bread and Butter Pudding.

Carrot Cake

For a more luxurious cake, double the icing, slice the cake in two, and fill the middle as well.

SERVES 8–10	20 MINS	45 MINS	8 WEEKS, UN-ICED

Special equipment
22cm (9in) round springform cake tin
zester

Ingredients
100g (3½oz) walnuts
225ml (7½fl oz) sunflower oil, plus extra for greasing
3 large eggs
225g (8oz) soft light brown sugar
1 tsp vanilla extract
200g (7oz) carrots, finely grated
100g (3½oz) sultanas

200g (7oz) self-raising flour
75g (2½oz) wholemeal self-raising flour
pinch of salt
1 tsp cinnamon
1 tsp ground ginger
¼ tsp finely grated nutmeg
finely grated zest of 1 orange

For the icing
50g (1¾oz) unsalted butter, softened
100g (3½oz) cream cheese, at room temperature
200g (7oz) icing sugar
½ tsp vanilla extract
2 oranges

1 Preheat the oven to 180°C (350°F/Gas 4). Bake the walnuts for 5 minutes, until light brown.

2 Put the nuts on a clean tea towel and rub them to remove excess skin. Set aside to cool.

3 Pour the oil and eggs into a large bowl, tip in the sugar, and add the vanilla.

4 Using an electric whisk, beat the oil mixture until it is lighter and noticeably thickened.

5 Squeeze the grated carrot thoroughly in a clean tea towel to remove excess liquid.

6 Gently fold the carrot into the cake batter, ensuring it is evenly blended throughout.

7 Chop the cooled walnuts roughly, leaving some large pieces.

8 Add the walnuts to the mixture, along with the sultanas, and gently fold them in.

9 Sift over the 2 types of flour, then tip in any bran remaining in the sieve.

10 Add the salt, spices, and orange zest, and fold all the ingredients together to combine.

11 Oil the tin and line with parchment. Pour in the cake mix and smooth with a palette knife.

12 Bake for 45 minutes. Test by inserting a skewer into the cake; it should come out clean.

13 If not, bake for a few more minutes and test again. Transfer to a wire rack to cool.

14 Combine the butter, cream cheese, icing sugar, and vanilla. Grate in the zest of 1 orange.

15 Using an electric whisk, mix all the ingredients until smooth, pale, and fluffy.

16 Using a palette knife, spread the icing over the cake. Make swirls for texture.

17 For additional decoration, zest the remaining orange using a zester tool.

18 Sprinkle the orange zest over the icing in an attractive pattern and transfer to a serving plate or cake stand. **STORE** The cake will keep in an airtight container for 3 days.

Carrot Cake variations

Courgette Cake

This intriguing alternative to carrot cake is a firm favourite.

| SERVES 8–10 | 20 MINS | 45 MINS | UP TO 8 WEEKS |

Special equipment
22cm (9in) round springform cake tin

Ingredients
225ml (7½fl oz) sunflower oil,
  plus extra for greasing
100g (3½oz) hazelnuts
3 large eggs
1 tsp vanilla extract
225g (8oz) caster sugar
200g (7oz) courgettes, finely grated
200g (7oz) self-raising flour
75g (2½oz) wholemeal self-raising flour
pinch of salt
1 tsp cinnamon
finely grated zest of 1 lemon

Method
1 Preheat the oven to 180°C (350°F/Gas 4). Oil the base and sides of the tin and line the base with baking parchment. Spread hazelnuts on a baking tray and cook for 5 minutes until lightly browned. Put the nuts on a clean tea towel and rub them to get rid of excess skin. Roughly chop and set aside.

2 Pour the oil and eggs into a bowl, add the vanilla, and tip in the sugar. Whisk the oil mixture until lighter and thickened. Squeeze moisture from the courgettes and fold in with the nuts. Sift over the flour, tipping any bran left in the sieve. Add the salt, cinnamon, and lemon zest, and fold.

3 Pour the batter into the tin. Bake for 45 minutes or until springy to the touch. Turn out onto a wire rack to cool completely.

STORE The cake will keep in an airtight container for 3 days.

BAKER'S TIP
Don't be put off by the unusual inclusion of courgettes. Courgettes are less sweet than carrots, but add moisture and a fresh flavour. The lack of icing makes this cake healthier.

Quick Carrot Cake

Carrot cakes are perfect for novice bakers as they do not require lengthy whisking or delicate folding. This variation is quick to prepare and guaranteed to disappear even faster.

SERVES 8 | 15 MINS | 20–25 MINS | 8 WEEKS, UN-ICED

Special equipment
20cm (8in) round springform cake tin

Ingredients
75g (2½oz) unsalted butter, melted and cooled, plus extra for greasing
75g (2½oz) wholemeal self-raising flour
1 tsp ground allspice
½ tsp ground ginger
½ tsp baking powder
2 carrots, coarsely grated
75g (2½oz) soft light brown sugar
50g (1¾oz) sultanas
2 eggs, beaten
3 tbsp fresh orange juice

For the icing
150g (5½oz) cream cheese, at room temperature
1 tbsp icing sugar
lemon zest, to decorate

Method
1 Preheat the oven to 190°C (375°F/Gas 5). Grease the cake tin and line the base with baking parchment.

2 Sift the flour, allspice, ginger, and baking powder into a large bowl, tipping in any bran that remains in the sieve. Add the carrots, sugar, and sultanas, then stir to mix. Add the eggs, 1 tablespoon of orange juice, and the butter. Stir until blended.

3 Pour the cake mix into the tin and level with a palette knife. Bake on a baking tray for 20 minutes or until a skewer inserted into the centre of the cake comes out clean. Let it stand in the tin for 10 minutes to cool.

4 Run a knife around the sides, invert onto a wire rack, peel off the paper, and leave to cool completely. Split the cake horizontally into 2 layers with a serrated knife.

5 For the icing, beat the cream cheese with the remaining orange juice and icing sugar. Spread the icing in the centre and over the top of the cake, and decorate with lemon zest.

STORE The cake will keep in an airtight container for 3 days.

Spiced Carrot Cake

This is a fabulous cake for winter, with hints of warming spice. Baking in a square tin allows the cake to be cut into bite-sized pieces, perfect for a party. **PICTURED OVERLEAF**

MAKES 16 SQUARES | 20 MINS | 30 MINS | 8 WEEKS, UN-ICED

Special equipment
20cm (8in) square cake tin

Ingredients
175g (6oz) self-raising flour
1 tsp cinnamon
1 tsp mixed spice
½ tsp bicarbonate of soda
100g (3½oz) light or dark soft brown sugar
150ml (5fl oz) sunflower oil
2 large eggs
75g (2½oz) golden syrup
125g (4½oz) carrots, coarsely grated
finely grated zest of 1 orange

For the icing
75g (2½oz) icing sugar
100g (3½oz) cream cheese, at room temperature
1–2 tbsp orange juice
finely grated zest of 1 orange, plus extra to decorate (optional)

Method
1 Preheat the oven to 180°C (350°F/Gas 4). Line the base and sides of the tin with parchment. In a bowl, mix the flour, spices, bicarbonate of soda, and sugar together.

2 In another bowl, mix the oil, eggs, and syrup, then combine with the dry ingredients. Stir in the carrot and orange zest, transfer to the tin and level the top.

3 Bake for 30 minutes or until firm to the touch. Leave in the tin for a few minutes, then turn out onto a wire rack to cool completely. Remove the baking parchment.

4 For the icing, sift the icing sugar into a bowl, add the cream cheese, orange juice, and orange zest. Beat with an electric whisk until spreadable. Spread the icing over the cake. Decorate with extra orange zest (if using), and cut into 16 squares to serve.

STORE The cake will keep in an airtight container for 3 days.

Lemon Polenta Cake

One of the few wheat-free cakes that work just as well as those made from wheat flour.

SERVES 6–8
30 MINS
50–60 MINS
UP TO 8 WEEKS

Special equipment
22cm (9in) round springform cake tin

Ingredients
175g (6oz) unsalted butter, softened, plus extra for greasing
200g (7oz) caster sugar
3 large eggs, beaten
75g (2½oz) polenta or coarse-ground cornmeal
175g (6oz) ground almonds
finely grated zest and juice of 2 lemons
1 tsp gluten-free baking powder
thick cream or crème fraîche, to serve (optional)

1 Preheat the oven to 160°C (325°F/Gas 3). Grease the tin, lining the base with parchment.

2 With an electric whisk, cream the butter and 175g (6oz) of the sugar until fluffy.

3 Gradually pour in the beaten eggs, a little at a time, whisking well after each addition.

4 Add the polenta and almonds, and gently fold into the mix using a metal spoon.

5 Finally, fold in the lemon zest and baking powder. The batter will seem quite stiff.

6 Scrape the mixture into the prepared tin and smooth the surface with a palette knife.

7 Bake the cake for 50–60 minutes until springy to the touch. It will not rise much.

8 Check the cake is cooked by inserting a skewer. The skewer should emerge clean.

9 Leave the cake in the tin for a few minutes until cool enough to handle.

EVERYDAY CAKES

10 Meanwhile, put the lemon juice and the remaining sugar in a small saucepan.

11 Heat the juice over medium heat until the sugar has completely dissolved. Take off heat.

12 Turn the cake out onto a wire rack, baked side upwards. Retain the parchment for now.

13 Using a thin skewer or cocktail stick, poke holes in the top of the cake while still warm.

14 Pour the hot lemon syrup a little at a time over the surface of the cake.

15 Only once the syrup has soaked into the cake, pour more on, until it is all used up.

16 Once cooled, serve the cake at room temperature on its own or with thick cream or crème fraîche. **STORE** The cake will keep in an airtight container for 3 days.

Wheat-free Cake variations

Chocolate and Brazil Nut Cake

This unusual wheat-free cake uses Brazil nuts instead of the typical almond and chocolate combination, to give a moist, rich finish to the cake.

| SERVES 6–8 | 25 MINS | 45–50 MINS | UP TO 4 WEEKS |

Special equipment
20cm (8in) round springform cake tin
food processor

Ingredients
75g (2½oz) unsalted butter, cubed, plus extra for greasing
100g (3½oz) good-quality dark chocolate, broken into pieces
150g (5½oz) Brazil nuts
125g (4½oz) caster sugar
4 large eggs, separated
cocoa powder or icing sugar, to serve
thick cream, to serve (optional)

Method
1 Preheat the oven to 180°C (350°F/Gas 4). Grease the cake tin and line the base with baking parchment. Melt the chocolate in a bowl over a little simmering water, and leave to cool.

2 In a food processor, grind the nuts and sugar finely. Add the butter and pulse until just blended (see Baker's Tip). Continue to blend while adding the egg yolks one at a time. Add the melted chocolate and blend.

3 In a separate bowl, whisk the egg whites to stiff peaks. Turn the chocolate mixture into a large bowl and beat in a few tablespoons of the egg whites to loosen it a little. Now carefully fold in the remaining egg whites with a large metal spoon.

4 Scrape the mixture into the tin and bake for 45–50 minutes until the surface is springy and a skewer inserted into the middle comes out clean. Allow to cool in the tin for a few minutes, then turn out onto a wire rack to cool completely. Remove the parchment. Sift over the cocoa powder or icing sugar. Serve with thick cream if you like.

STORE The cake will keep in an airtight container for 3 days.

BAKER'S TIP
Care should be taken to pulse the butter into the nut and sugar mixture in short bursts, as prolonged processing will result in the natural oils in the nuts being released, which would give the finished cake an oily flavour.

Torta margherita

This light and lemony Italian classic is made with potato flour.

| SERVES 6–8 | 20 MINS | 25–30 MINS | UP TO 8 WEEKS |

Special equipment
20cm (8in) round springform cake tin

Ingredients
25g (scant 1oz) unsalted butter, plus extra for greasing
2 large eggs, plus 1 egg yolk
100g (3½oz) caster sugar
½ tsp vanilla extract
100g (3½oz) potato flour, sifted
½ tsp gluten-free baking powder
finely grated zest of ½ lemon
icing sugar, for dusting

Method
1 Melt the butter and set aside to cool. Preheat the oven to 180°C (350°F/Gas 4). Grease the tin and line the base with baking parchment.

2 In a large bowl, whisk the eggs, egg yolk, sugar, and vanilla extract together for about 5 minutes until thick, pale, and at least doubled in volume. Gently fold in the potato flour, baking powder, and lemon zest, then fold in the melted butter.

3 Scrape the batter into the prepared tin and bake for 25–30 minutes until the surface is golden brown and springy to the touch. A skewer inserted into the middle should come out clean.

4 Leave the cake to cool for 10 minutes in its tin, then turn out to cool completely on a wire rack. Remove the baking parchment. Dust with icing sugar to serve.

STORE The torta will keep in an airtight container for 2 days.

Castagnaccio

Chestnut flour gives this interesting cake a dense yet moist texture.

SERVES	25	50–60
6–8	MINS	MINS

Special equipment
20cm (8in) round springform cake tin

Ingredients
1 tbsp olive oil, plus extra for greasing
50g (1¾oz) raisins
25g (scant 1oz) flaked almonds
30g (1oz) pine nuts
300g (10½oz) chestnut flour
25g (scant 1oz) caster sugar
pinch of salt
400ml (14fl oz) milk or water
1 tbsp finely chopped rosemary leaves
1 orange, zested

Method

1 Preheat the oven to 180°C (350°F/Gas 4). Grease the cake tin and line the base with baking parchment. Cover the raisins with warm water and leave for 5 minutes to plump them up. Drain.

2 Put the almonds and pine nuts on a baking tray and bake in the oven for 5–10 minutes until lightly browned. Sift the chestnut flour into a large mixing bowl. Add the sugar and salt.

3 Using a balloon whisk, gradually whisk in the milk or water to produce a thick, smooth batter. Whisk in the olive oil, pour the batter into the tin, and scatter over the raisins, rosemary, orange zest, and nuts.

4 Bake at the centre of the oven for 50–60 minutes until the surface is dry and the edges slightly browned. The cake will not really rise. Leave in the tin for 10 minutes, then carefully turn it out onto a wire rack and leave it to cool completely. Remove the baking parchment and serve.

STORE The cake will keep in an airtight container for 3 days.

NOTE Chestnut flour is available from Italian delis, health food stores, or online.

Chocolate Cake

Everyone loves a classic chocolate cake, and in this version the yogurt in the mix makes it extra moist.

SERVES 6–8 | **30 MINS** | **20–25 MINS** | **8 WEEKS, UNFILLED**

Special equipment
2 x 17cm (6¾in) round cake tins

Ingredients
175g (6oz) unsalted butter, softened,
  plus extra for greasing
175g (6oz) soft light brown sugar
3 large eggs
125g (4½oz) self-raising flour
50g (1¾oz) cocoa powder
1 tsp baking powder
2 tbsp Greek yogurt
  or thick plain yogurt

For the chocolate buttercream
50g (1¾oz) unsalted butter, softened
75g (2½oz) icing sugar, sifted,
  plus extra to serve
25g (scant 1oz) cocoa powder
a little milk, if needed

1 Preheat the oven to 180°C (350°F/Gas 4). Grease the tins and line with parchment.

2 Chop the butter and place it in a large bowl with the sugar.

3 With an electric whisk, cream the butter mixture until light and fluffy.

4 Drop in the eggs one at a time, beating after each addition, until well combined.

5 In a separate large bowl, sift together the flour, cocoa powder, and baking powder.

6 Fold the flour mixture into the cake batter until well blended, trying to keep volume.

7 Gently fold through the thick yogurt. This will help to make the cake moist.

8 Divide the mixture between the 2 cake tins, smoothing the surfaces with a palette knife.

9 Bake in the middle of the oven for 20–25 minutes until risen and springy to the touch.

10 A skewer inserted into the middle should come out clean. If not, bake a little more.

11 Leave the sponges in their tins for a few minutes. Remove the parchment and cool.

12 For the buttercream, place the butter, icing sugar, and cocoa powder in a large bowl.

13 Blend the buttercream together with an electric whisk for 5 minutes or until fluffy.

14 If the cream is stiff, add milk, 1 teaspoon at a time, until it has a spreading consistency.

15 Spread the base of one sponge with the buttercream, then top with the other sponge.

16 Transfer the cake to a serving plate and sift a little icing sugar evenly over the top, to serve.
STORE The cake will keep in an airtight container for 2 days.

Chocolate Cake variations

Triple-Layer Chocolate Cake

Moist sponge, fluffy vanilla cream, and smooth chocolate icing – everything a chocolate and cake lover could wish for.

SERVES 12 | 15 MINS | 30–35 MINS

Special equipment
3 x 20cm (8in) round cake tins

Ingredients
300g (10oz) self-raising flour
4 tbsp cocoa powder
1 heaped tsp bicarbonate of soda
300g (10oz) unsalted butter, softened, plus 2 tbsp and extra for greasing
300g (10oz) golden caster sugar, plus 1 tbsp
5 large eggs
1 tsp vanilla extract, plus a few drops
4 tbsp milk
175g (6oz) plain chocolate
450ml (15fl oz) double cream

Method
1 Preheat the oven to 180°C (350°F/Gas 4). Lightly grease the cake tins and line the bases with baking parchment. Sift the flour, cocoa, and baking soda together into a bowl. Cream the butter and sugar in a separate bowl with an electric whisk until pale and fluffy.

2 Add the sifted flour, eggs, vanilla, and milk, then beat for 1 minute, until the mixture is uniform and fluffy. Divide evenly between the 3 cake tins and level the tops. Bake in the oven for 30–35 minutes. Leave the cakes to cool in the tins for 5 minutes, then turn them out on to a wire rack, and leave until cold.

3 Break off 50g (2oz) of the chocolate and push a vegetable peeler across the surface to form curls. Set aside in a cool place.

4 Measure 150ml (5fl oz) of the cream into a heatproof bowl. Break the remaining chocolate into squares and add to the bowl. Place over a pan of gently simmering water, making sure the base of the bowl doesn't touch the water, and stir until the chocolate melts and a smooth shiny icing forms. Remove from the heat, stir in 2 tablespoons butter, and leave to cool.

5 Pour the remaining cream into a bowl, add 1 tablespoon sugar, a few drops of vanilla, and whisk until soft peaks form. Divide the cream between 2 of the cakes, stack them on top of each other, then cover with the third cake. Spoon the cooled icing over the top, letting it run down the sides. Sprinkle with the chocolate curls, and serve.

Chocolate Cake with Fudge Icing

Always a popular choice, this one is a must for your cake repertoire.

SERVES 8–12 | 20 MINS | 40 MINS | 8 WEEKS, UN-ICED

Special equipment
2 x 20cm (8in) round cake tins

Ingredients
225g (8oz) unsalted butter, softened, plus extra for greasing
200g (7oz) self-raising flour
25g (scant 1oz) cocoa powder
4 large eggs
225g (8oz) caster sugar
1 tsp vanilla extract
1 tsp baking powder

For the icing
45g (1½oz) cocoa powder
150g (5½oz) icing sugar
45g (1½oz) unsalted butter, melted
3 tbsp milk, plus extra to slacken the mixture

Method
1 Preheat the oven to 180°C (350°F/Gas 4). Grease the tins, then line the bases with baking parchment. Sift the flour and cocoa powder into a bowl, and add all the other cake ingredients. Whisk together with an electric whisk for a few minutes until well combined. Whisk in 2 tablespoons of warm water so the mixture is soft. Divide evenly between the tins, and smooth the tops.

2 Bake for 35–40 minutes or until risen and firm to the touch. Leave to cool for a few minutes before turning out onto wire racks to cool completely. Remove the parchment.

3 For the icing, sift the cocoa powder and icing sugar into a bowl, add the butter and milk, and whisk until smooth and well combined. Add a little extra milk if the mixture is too thick; you need to be able to spread it easily. Spread over the tops of the cooled cakes, then sandwich together.

STORE The cake will keep for 2 days in an airtight container.

Pear and Chocolate Cake

This rich, luscious cake is a good choice when you want to impress.

SERVES   **15**   **30**
6–8   **MINS**   **MINS**

Special equipment
20cm (8in) round springform cake tin

Ingredients
125g (4½oz) unsalted butter, softened,
  plus extra for greasing
175g (6oz) golden caster sugar
4 large eggs, lightly beaten
250g (9oz) wholemeal self-raising flour, sifted
50g (1¾oz) cocoa powder, sifted
50g (1¾oz) good-quality dark chocolate,
  broken into pieces (see Baker's Tip)
2 pears, peeled, cored, and chopped
150ml (5fl oz) milk
icing sugar, for dusting

Method
1 Preheat the oven to 180°C (350°F/Gas 4). Line the base of the cake tin with baking parchment and grease the sides with butter.

2 Cream the butter with the sugar using an electric whisk until pale and creamy. Beat the eggs in gradually, adding a little of the flour each time until all of it is combined. Fold in the cocoa powder, chocolate, and pears. Add the milk to the mixture and combine.

3 Pour the cake mixture into the prepared tin, place it in the oven, and bake for about 30 minutes or until firm and springy to the touch. Allow to cool in the tin for 5 minutes, then remove the tin, and transfer the cake to a wire rack to cool completely. Remove the baking parchment. Sift over icing sugar before serving.

STORE The cake will keep in an airtight container for 2 days.

Devil's Food Cake

This American classic uses the flavour of coffee to enhance the richness of the chocolate, adding a wonderful depth of flavour to the finished cake.

| SERVES 8–10 | 30 MINS | 30–35 MINS | 8 WEEKS, UNFILLED |

Special equipment
2 x 20cm (8in) round cake tins

Ingredients
100g (3½oz) unsalted butter, softened, plus extra for greasing
275g (9½oz) caster sugar
2 large eggs
200g (7oz) self-raising flour
75g (2½oz) cocoa powder
1 tsp baking powder
1 tbsp coffee powder mixed with 125ml (4fl oz) boiling water, or equivalent cooled espresso
125ml (4fl oz) milk
1 tsp vanilla extract

For the frosting
125g (4½oz) unsalted butter, diced
25g (scant 1oz) cocoa powder
125g (4½oz) icing sugar
2–3 tbsp milk
dark or milk chocolate, for the shavings

Method

1 Preheat the oven to 180°C (350°F/Gas 4). Grease the cake tins and line the bases with baking parchment. Using an electric whisk, cream together the butter and sugar until light and fluffy.

2 Beat in the eggs one at a time, whisking well after each addition, until well mixed. In a separate bowl, sift together the flour, cocoa powder, and baking powder. In another bowl, mix together the cooled coffee, milk, and vanilla extract.

3 Beat alternate spoonfuls of the dry and liquid ingredients into the cake batter. Once the mixture is well blended, divide it between the tins.

4 Bake for 30–35 minutes until the cakes are springy to the touch and a skewer inserted into the middle comes out clean. Leave to cool in the tins for a few minutes, then turn out onto a wire rack to cool completely. Remove the baking parchment.

5 For the frosting, melt the butter in a pan over low heat. Add the cocoa powder and continue to cook for a minute or two, stirring frequently. Allow to cool slightly.

6 Sift in the icing sugar, beating thoroughly to combine. Blend in the milk 1 tablespoon at a time, until smooth and glossy. Allow to cool (it will thicken) and then use half to sandwich the cakes together, and the remainder to decorate the top and sides of the cake. Finally, use a vegetable peeler to create chocolate shavings and scatter them evenly over the top of the cake.

STORE This cake will keep in an airtight container in a cool place for 5 days.

BAKER'S TIP
Don't be put off by the inclusion of coffee in this recipe. Even if you don't normally like coffee-flavoured cakes, you should use it here. It results in a deep, dark fudgy texture and also subtly enhances the chocolate flavour, rather than giving an overt coffee taste.

EVERYDAY CAKES

Chocolate Fudge Cake

Everyone should have a chocolate fudge cake recipe, and this one is a winner. The oil and syrup keep it moist, and the icing is a classic.

SERVES 6–8	40 MINS	30 MINS	8 WEEKS, UNFILLED

Special equipment
2 x 17cm (6¾in) round cake tins

Ingredients
150ml (5fl oz) sunflower oil,
  plus extra for greasing
175g (6oz) self-raising flour
25g (scant 1oz) cocoa powder
1 tsp baking powder
150g (5½oz) soft light brown sugar
3 tbsp golden syrup
2 eggs
150ml (5fl oz) milk

For the icing
125g (4½oz) unsalted butter
25g (scant 1oz) cocoa powder
125g (4½oz) icing sugar
2 tbsp milk, if necessary

Method

1 Preheat the oven to 180°C (350°F/Gas 4). Grease the tins and line the bases with baking parchment. In a large bowl, sift together the flour, cocoa, and baking powder. Mix in the sugar.

2 Gently heat the golden syrup until runny and leave to cool. In a separate bowl, beat the eggs, sunflower oil, and milk together using an electric whisk.

3 Whisk the egg mixture into the flour mixture until well combined. Gently fold in the syrup and divide the batter between the cake tins.

4 Bake the cakes in the middle of the oven for 30 minutes or until springy to the touch, and a skewer inserted into the middle comes out clean. Leave to cool slightly in the tins, then turn out onto a wire rack to cool completely. Remove the parchment.

5 To make the icing, melt the butter over low heat. Stir in the cocoa powder and cook gently for 1–2 minutes, then leave to cool completely. Sift the icing sugar into a bowl.

6 Pour the melted butter and cocoa into the icing sugar and beat together to combine. If the mixture seems a little dry, add the milk, 1 tablespoon at a time, until the icing is smooth and glossy. Leave to cool for up to 30 minutes. It will thicken as it cools.

7 When thick, use half the icing to fill the cake and the other half to top it.

STORE This cake will keep in an airtight container for 3 days.

> ### BAKER'S TIP
> The icing used here is a real staple, and can be used to finish many chocolate recipes. Leftovers that are slightly old can be heated for 30 seconds in a microwave. The icing will melt into a rich, fudgy sauce, and the cake can be served with vanilla ice cream for a delicious, quick dessert.

Baked Chocolate Mousse

This classic mousse is easy to make, even for a novice. Slice the moist mousse with a sharp knife dipped in hot water, and wipe between cuts.

SERVES 8–12   **20 MINS**   **1 HOUR**

Special equipment
23cm (9in) round springform cake tin

Ingredients

250g (9oz) unsalted butter, cubed
350g (12oz) good-quality dark chocolate, broken into pieces
250g (9oz) light soft brown sugar
5 large eggs, separated
pinch of salt
cocoa powder or icing sugar, for dusting
thick cream, to serve (optional)

Method

1 Preheat the oven to 180°C (350°F/Gas 4). Line the base of the tin with parchment. Set a heatproof bowl over a pan of simmering water (make sure the base of the bowl does not touch the water), and melt the butter and chocolate together until smooth and glossy, lightly stirring to combine.

2 Remove from the pan and allow to cool slightly, then stir in the sugar, followed by the egg yolks, one at a time.

3 Put the egg whites in a mixing bowl with the salt, and beat with an electric whisk until soft peaks form. Gradually fold into the chocolate mixture, then pour into the cake tin, and smooth the top.

4 Bake for 1 hour, or until the top is firm but the middle still wobbles slightly when you shake the tin. Leave to cool completely in the tin. Remove the baking parchment. Dust with cocoa powder or icing sugar before serving with a dollop of thick cream.

BAKER'S TIP

To give a deliciously moist, almost gooey finish to this recipe, take care not to overcook the cake. The centre should be only just set when it is taken out of the oven, and when the mousse is pressed gently with a finger it should hold the impression and not spring back.

German Apple Cake

This simple apple cake is transformed into something special with a delicious, crumbly streusel topping.

SERVES 6–8

30 MINS

45–50 MINS

Chilling time
30 mins

Special equipment
20cm (8in) loose-bottomed cake tin

Ingredients
175g (6oz) unsalted butter, softened, plus extra for greasing
175g (6oz) light muscovado sugar
finely grated zest of 1 lemon
3 eggs, lightly beaten
175g (6oz) self-raising flour
3 tbsp milk
2 tart dessert apples, peeled, cored, and cut into even, slim wedges

For the streusel topping
115g (4oz) plain flour
85g (3oz) light muscovado sugar
2 tsp ground cinnamon
85g (3oz) unsalted butter, diced

1 To make the topping, put the flour, sugar, and cinnamon in a mixing bowl.

2 Rub in the butter gently with your fingertips to form a crumbly ball of dough.

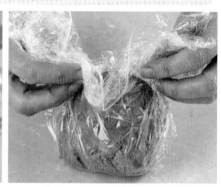

3 Wrap the streusel dough in cling film and chill in the refrigerator for 30 minutes.

4 Preheat the oven to 190°C (375°F/Gas 5). Grease the tin and line with baking parchment.

5 Put the butter and sugar in a bowl, and whisk until pale and creamy.

6 Add the lemon zest and whisk slowly until well dispersed through the batter.

7 Beat in the eggs, a little at a time, mixing well after each addition to avoid curdling.

8 Sift the flour into the batter and gently fold in with a metal spoon.

9 Finally, add the milk to the batter and gently mix it in.

10 Spread half the mixture in the prepared tin and smooth the surface with a palette knife.

11 Arrange half the apple wedges over the batter, reserving the best pieces for the top.

12 Spread the rest of the mixture over the apples. Smooth once more with a palette knife.

13 Arrange the remaining apple wedges on top of the cake in an attractive pattern.

14 Remove the streusel dough from the refrigerator and coarsely grate it.

15 Sprinkle the grated streusel evenly over the top of the cake.

16 Bake in the centre of the oven for 45 minutes. Insert a skewer into the centre.

17 If the skewer emerges coated in batter, cook for a few minutes more and test again.

18 Leave the cake in the tin for 10 minutes. Keeping the streusel on top, carefully remove the cake from the tin and cool on a wire rack. Serve warm.

Apple Cake variations

Apple, Sultana, and Pecan Cake

Sometimes I like a healthier cake. This cake uses little fat and is stuffed full of fruit and nuts, making it a virtuous yet delicious choice.

SERVES 10–12	25 MINS	30–35 MINS

Special equipment
23cm (9in) round springform cake tin

Ingredients
butter, for greasing
50g (1¾oz) shelled pecan nuts
200g (7oz) apples, peeled, cored, and finely diced
150g (5½oz) soft light brown sugar
250g (9oz) self-raising flour
1 tsp baking powder
2 tsp cinnamon
pinch of salt
3½ tbsp sunflower oil
3½ tbsp milk, plus extra if necessary
2 eggs
1 tsp vanilla extract
50g (1¾oz) sultanas
whipped cream or icing sugar, to serve (optional)

Method
1 Preheat the oven to 180°C (350°F/Gas 4). Grease the tin and line the base with baking parchment. Place the nuts on a baking sheet and toast them in the oven for 5 minutes until crisp. Cool and roughly chop.

2 In a large bowl, mix the apples and sugar together. Sift over the flour, baking powder, cinnamon, and salt, and fold in. In a jug, whisk together the oil, milk, eggs, and vanilla extract.

3 Pour the milk into the cake mixture and stir until well combined. Fold in the pecans and sultanas, and pour into the prepared tin.

4 Bake in the centre of the oven for 30–35 minutes, until a skewer comes out clean. Leave to cool for a few minutes in the tin, then turn out onto a wire rack. Remove the baking parchment. Serve warm with whipped cream as a dessert, or cooled and dusted with icing sugar.

STORE The cake will keep in an airtight container for 3 days.

Torta di mela

A firm dessert apple is best for this moist and dense Italian cake.

SERVES 8	20–25 MINS	1¼–1½ HOURS	UP TO 8 WEEKS

Special equipment
23–25cm (9–10in) round springform cake tin

Ingredients
175g (6oz) unsalted butter, softened, plus extra for greasing
175g (6oz) plain flour, plus extra for dusting
½ tsp salt
1 tsp baking powder
finely grated zest and juice of 1 lemon
625g (1lb 5oz) apples, peeled, cored, and sliced
200g (7oz) caster sugar, plus 60g (2oz) for glazing
2 eggs
4 tbsp milk

Method
1 Preheat the oven to 180°C (350°F/Gas 4). Grease the tin and sprinkle with a little flour. Sift the flour with the salt and baking powder. Pour the lemon juice over the apple slices.

2 With an electric whisk, beat the butter in a large bowl until soft and creamy. Add the sugar and zest, and beat until light and fluffy. Add the eggs one at a time, beating well after each addition. Gradually whisk in the milk until the batter is smooth.

3 Fold in the flour mix and half the apples, spoon into the tin, and smooth the top. Place the remaining apple slices in concentric circles on top. Bake for 1¼–1½ hours, until a skewer comes out clean; it will still be moist.

4 Meanwhile, make the glaze. Heat 4 tablespoons of water and the remaining sugar in a pan over low heat until the sugar has dissolved. Bring to a boil and simmer for 2 minutes, without stirring. Let it cool.

5 Brush the glaze over the top of the cake as soon as it comes out of the oven. Let the cake cool in the tin, then transfer to a serving plate.

STORE The cake will keep in an airtight container for 2 days.

Toffee Apple Cake

Caramelizing the apples in this cake gives them a wonderful toffee apple taste, and soaking the cake in the buttery cooking juices after baking makes it especially moist and flavoursome.

| SERVES 8–10 | 40 MINS | 40–45 MINS | UP TO 4 WEEKS |

Special equipment
22cm (9in) round springform cake tin

Ingredients
200g (7oz) unsalted butter, softened, plus extra for greasing
50g (1¾oz) caster sugar
250g (9oz) apples, peeled, cored, and diced
150g (5½oz) soft light brown sugar
3 eggs
150g (5½oz) self-raising flour
1 heaped tsp baking powder
whipped cream or icing sugar, to serve (optional)

Method

1 Preheat the oven to 180°C (350°F/Gas 4). Grease the tin and line the base with baking parchment. In a large frying pan, gently heat 50g (1¾oz) of the butter and the caster sugar until melted and golden brown. Add the diced apple and fry gently for 7–8 minutes until they start to soften and caramelize.

2 With an electric whisk, cream together the remaining butter and brown sugar in a bowl until light and fluffy. Add the eggs one at a time, beating well after each addition. Sift the flour and baking powder together, and gently fold into the mixture.

3 Remove the apples from the pan with a slotted spoon and set aside the pan with the juices to use later. Scatter the apples over the base of the tin. Spoon the batter on top, then place the tin on a baking tray, with sides to catch any drips, and bake in the centre of the oven for 40–45 minutes. Leave to cool for a few minutes, then turn out onto a wire rack.

4 Put the frying pan with the leftover juices back on low heat, and heat gently until warmed through. With a fine skewer or wooden cocktail stick, make holes over the surface of the cake. Put the cake on a plate and pour over the apple syrup, letting it soak in. Serve warm with whipped cream, or cooled and dusted with icing sugar.

STORE The cake will keep in an airtight container for 3 days.

Rhubarb and Ginger Upside Down Cake

Young rhubarb is cooked into a simple upside down cake to give a modern twist on a classic dessert.

SERVES 6–8 | **40 MINS** | **40–45 MINS**

Special equipment
22cm (9in) round springform cake tin

Ingredients
150g (5½oz) unsalted butter,
　softened, plus extra for greasing
500g (1lb 2oz) young, pink rhubarb
150g (5½oz) soft dark brown sugar
4 tbsp finely chopped, preserved
　stem ginger
3 large eggs
150g (5½oz) self-raising flour

2 tsp ground ginger
1 tsp baking powder
double cream, whipped, or
　crème fraîche, to serve (optional)

1 Preheat the oven to 180°C (350°F/Gas 4). Melt a little butter and brush to grease the tin.

2 Line the base and sides of the cake tin with baking parchment.

3 Wash the rhubarb, removing discoloured pieces and the dry ends of the stalks.

4 Cut the rhubarb into 2cm (¾in) lengths with a sharp knife that will cut through the strings.

5 Scatter a little of the sugar evenly over the base of the cake tin.

6 Now scatter half the chopped ginger evenly over the base of the tin.

7 Lay the rhubarb in the tin, tightly packed, making sure the base is well covered.

8 Place the butter and remaining sugar into a large bowl.

9 With an electric whisk, cream the butter and sugar until light and fluffy.

54

10 Beat in the eggs one at a time, whisking as much air as possible into the mixture.

11 Gently fold the remaining chopped ginger into the batter, until well dispersed.

12 Sift together the flour, ground ginger, and baking powder into a separate bowl.

13 Add the sifted ingredients to the bowl containing the cake batter.

14 Gently fold the dry ingredients into the cake batter, keeping volume in the batter.

15 Spoon the cake batter over the base, being careful not to disturb the rhubarb.

16 Bake the cake in the centre of the oven for 45 minutes until springy to the touch.

17 Leave the cake to cool in its tin for 20–30 minutes, before carefully turning it out.

18 Serve warm as a dessert with whipped cream or crème fraîche. **STORE** The cake is also good cold and will keep in a cool place in an airtight container for 2 days.

Fresh Fruit Cake variations

Blueberry Upside Down Cake

This is an unusual yet delicious way of turning a punnet of blueberries and a few storecupboard essentials into a quick and delicious dessert for a crowd.

SERVES
8–10

15 MINS

40 MINS

Special equipment
22cm (9in) round springform cake tin

Ingredients
150g (5½oz) unsalted butter, softened, plus extra for greasing
150g (5½oz) caster sugar
3 eggs
1 tsp vanilla extract
100g (3½oz) self-raising flour
1 tsp baking powder
50g (1¾oz) ground almonds
250g (9oz) fresh blueberries
cream or vanilla custard, or icing sugar, to serve (optional)

Method

1 Preheat the oven to 180°C (350°F/Gas 4) and place a baking sheet inside. Grease the cake tin and line the base with baking parchment. Cream together the butter and sugar using an electric whisk, until light and fluffy.

2 Gradually beat in the eggs and vanilla extract, whisking well between each addition, until well combined. Sift together the flour and baking powder, add the ground almonds, and fold into the batter.

3 Tip the blueberries into the tin and spread the batter gently over them. Bake the cake on the baking sheet in the centre of the oven for 35–40 minutes until golden brown and springy to the touch; a skewer should come out clean. Leave to cool for a few minutes, before removing from the tin.

4 Place the cake on a serving plate. Serve warm as a dessert, topped with cream or light vanilla custard; or serve cold, dusted with icing sugar.

STORE The cake will keep for 2 days in an airtight container.

Pear Cake

Fresh pear, yogurt, and almonds make this a very moist cake.

SERVES
6–8

40 MINS

45–50 MINS

UP TO 8 WEEKS

Special equipment
18cm (7in) round springform cake tin

Ingredients
100g (3½oz) unsalted butter, softened, plus extra for greasing
75g (2½oz) soft light brown sugar
1 egg, lightly beaten
125g (4½oz) self-raising flour
1 tsp baking powder
½ tsp ground ginger
½ tsp cinnamon
finely grated zest and juice of ½ orange
4 tbsp Greek yogurt or soured cream
25g (scant 1oz) ground almonds
1 large or 2 small pears, peeled, cored, and sliced

For the topping
2 tbsp flaked almonds, lightly toasted
2 tbsp demerara sugar

Method

1 Preheat the oven to 180°C (350°F/Gas 4). Grease the cake tin and line the base with baking parchment. Whisk together the butter and sugar until light and fluffy. Beat the egg into the creamed mixture.

2 Sift together the flour, baking powder, ginger, and cinnamon, and very gently fold into the batter mixture. Fold in the orange zest and juice, yogurt or soured cream, and the ground almonds. Pour half the batter into the tin. Top with the pears and cover with rest of the batter.

3 In a small bowl, toss together the flaked almonds and demerara sugar. Sprinkle the mixture over the top of the cake and bake in the centre of the oven for 45–50 minutes until a skewer comes out clean.

4 Leave the cake to cool in its tin for about 10 minutes, then turn it out onto a wire rack to cool. Serve warm or at room temperature.

STORE The cake will keep in a cool place in an airtight container for 3 days.

Cherry and Almond Cake

A classic combination of flavours, and always popular with guests.

| SERVES 8–10 | 20 MINS | 1½–1¾ HOURS | UP TO 4 WEEKS |

Special equipment
20cm (8in) deep round springform cake tin

Ingredients
150g (5½oz) unsalted butter, softened, plus extra for greasing
150g (5½oz) caster sugar
2 large eggs, lightly beaten
250g (9oz) self-raising flour, sifted
1 tsp baking powder
150g (5½oz) ground almonds
1 tsp vanilla extract
75ml (2½fl oz) whole milk
400g (14oz) pitted cherries
25g (scant 1oz) blanched almonds, chopped

Method

1 Preheat the oven to 180°C (350°F/Gas 4). Grease the tin and line the base with baking parchment. In a bowl, whisk the butter and sugar until creamy. Beat in the eggs one at a time, adding a tablespoon of flour to the mixture before adding the second egg.

2 Mix in the remaining flour, baking powder, ground almonds, vanilla extract, and milk. Mix in half the cherries, then spoon the mixture into the tin and smooth the top. Scatter the remaining cherries and almonds over the surface.

3 Bake for 1½–1¾ hours or until golden brown and firm to the touch. A skewer inserted into the cake should come out clean. If the surface of the cake starts to brown before it is fully cooked, cover with foil. When cooked, leave to cool in the tin for a few minutes, then remove the foil and parchment, and transfer to a wire rack to cool completely before serving.

STORE This cake will keep in an airtight container for 2 days.

Bavarian Plum Cake

Bavaria is famous for its sweet baking. This unusual cake is a cross between a sweet bread and a custardy fruit tart.

SERVES 8–10	35–40 MINS	50–55 MINS	UP TO 4 WEEKS

Rising and proving time
2–2¾ hrs

Special equipment
28cm (11in) tart tin

Ingredients
1½ tsp dried yeast
vegetable oil, for greasing
375g (13oz) plain flour, plus extra for dusting
2 tbsp caster sugar
1 tsp salt
3 eggs
125g (4½oz) unsalted butter, softened,
   plus extra for greasing

For the filling
2 tbsp dried breadcrumbs
875g (1lb 12½oz) purple plums,
   stoned and quartered
2 egg yolks
100g (3½oz) caster sugar
60ml (2fl oz) double cream

Method

1 Sprinkle the yeast over 60ml (2fl oz) lukewarm water in a small bowl. Let stand for 5 minutes until dissolved. Lightly oil another bowl. Sift the flour onto a work surface. Make a well in the centre and add the sugar, salt, yeast mixture, and eggs.

2 Work the flour to form a soft dough; adding more flour if it is very sticky. Knead on a floured work surface for 10 minutes until elastic. Work in more flour as needed so that the dough is slightly sticky but peels away easily from the work surface.

3 Add the butter to the dough; pinch and squeeze to mix it in, then knead until smooth. Shape into a ball and put it into the oiled bowl. Cover, and let rise in the refrigerator for 1½–2 hours, or overnight, until doubled in size.

4 Grease the tart tin. Knead the chilled brioche dough lightly to knock out the air. Flour the work surface; roll out the dough into a 32cm (13in) round. Wrap the dough around the rolling pin and loosely drape it over the dish. Press the dough into the dish and cut off any excess.

5 Sprinkle the breadcrumbs over the dough. Arrange the plum wedges, cut side up, in concentric circles on the brioche shell. Let stand at room temperature for 30–45 minutes until the edge of the dough is puffed. Meanwhile, preheat the oven to 220°C (425°F/Gas 7) and put a baking sheet in the oven to heat up.

6 For the custard mixture, place the egg yolks and two-thirds of the sugar into a bowl. Pour in the double cream, whisk together, and set aside.

7 Sprinkle the plums with the remaining sugar. Transfer the tart to the warmed baking sheet and cook in the oven for 5 minutes. Remove from the oven and reduce the heat to 180°C (350°F/Gas 4).

8 Ladle the custard mixture over the fruit and return to the oven. Continue baking for about 45 minutes until the dough is browned, the fruit tender, and the custard is just set. Let it cool on a wire rack. Serve warm or at room temperature.

STORE The cake will keep in an airtight container in the refrigerator for 2 days.

BAKER'S TIP

Baked custard should never be completely set when it is taken from the oven. Instead, there should always be a slight wobble in the middle when the tin is shaken, or the custard will be rubbery and hard, rather than unctuous and yielding.

Banana Bread

A mash of ripe bananas is delicious baked in this sweet quick bread. Spices and nuts add flavour and crunch.

MAKES 2 LOAVES | **20–25 MINS** | **35–40 MINS** | **UP TO 8 WEEKS**

Special equipment
2 x 450g (1lb) loaf tins

Ingredients
unsalted butter, for greasing
375g (13oz), strong white bread flour, plus extra for dusting
2 tsp baking powder
2 tsp cinnamon
1 tsp salt
125g (4½oz) walnut pieces, coarsely chopped

3 eggs
3 ripe bananas, peeled and chopped
finely grated zest and juice of 1 lemon
125ml (4fl oz) vegetable oil
200g (7oz) granulated sugar
100g (3½oz) soft brown sugar
2 tsp vanilla extract
cream cheese or butter, to serve (optional)

1 Preheat the oven to 180°C (350°F, Gas 4). Grease each of the loaf tins thoroughly.

2 Sprinkle 2–3 tablespoons of flour into each tin. Turn to coat and tap to remove excess flour.

3 Sift the flour, baking powder, cinnamon, and salt into a large bowl. Mix in the walnuts.

4 Make a well in the centre of the flour mixture for the wet ingredients.

5 Beat the eggs in a separate bowl with a fork or hand whisk.

6 Mash the bananas with a fork in another bowl, until they form a smooth paste.

7 Stir the bananas into the egg mixture until well blended. Add the lemon zest and mix.

8 Add the oil, granulated and brown sugars, vanilla, and lemon juice. Stir until combined.

9 Pour three-quarters of the banana mixture into the well in the flour, and stir well.

10 Gradually blend in the dry ingredients, adding the remaining banana mixture.

11 Stir until just smooth; if the batter is over-mixed, the banana bread will be tough.

12 Spoon the batter into the tins, dividing it equally. The tins should be about half full.

13 Bake for 35–40 minutes until the loaves start to shrink away from the sides of the tins.

14 Test each loaf with a skewer inserted into the centre; it should come out clean.

15 Let the loaves cool slightly, then transfer to a wire rack to cool completely.

16 Serve the banana bread sliced and spread with cream cheese or butter. It is also good toasted. **STORE** This bread will keep in an airtight container for 3–4 days.

Loaf Cake variations

EVERYDAY CAKES

Apple Loaf Cake

Here apples and wholemeal flour make for a healthier cake.

| MAKES 1 LOAF | 30 MINS | 40–50 MINS | UP TO 8 WEEKS |

Special equipment
900g (2lb) loaf tin

Ingredients
120g (4oz) unsalted butter, softened, plus extra for greasing
60g (2oz) soft light brown sugar
60g (2oz) caster sugar
2 eggs
1 tsp vanilla extract
60g (2oz) self-raising flour, plus extra for tossing
60g (2oz) wholemeal self-raising flour
1 tsp baking powder
2 tsp cinnamon
2 apples, peeled, cored, and diced

Method
1 Preheat the oven to 180°C (350°F/Gas 4). Grease the tin and line the base with baking parchment. In a bowl, whisk together the butter and the sugars.

2 Beat in the eggs, one at a time. Add the vanilla extract. In a separate bowl, sift together the flours, baking powder, and cinnamon. Fold the dry ingredients into the batter, mixing well.

3 Toss the apples in a little self-raising flour, then fold them into the batter. Pour the mixture into the tin. Bake in the centre of the oven for 40–50 minutes until the cake is golden brown. Leave to cool slightly, then turn out onto a wire rack.

STORE The cake will keep in an airtight container for 3 days.

BAKER'S TIP
When baking with any dried or fresh fruit, toss it lightly in flour before adding it to the wet ingredients. This floury coating will help stop the fruit from sinking to the bottom of the cake while cooking, ensuring it stays evenly distributed throughout.

Pecan and Cranberry Loaf Cake

Dried cranberries make a novel alternative to the more usual sultanas or raisins, adding sweet and sharp notes to this wholesome cake. ▶

| MAKES 1 LOAF | 30 MINS | 50–60 MINS | UP TO 4 WEEKS |

Special equipment
900g (2lb) loaf tin

Ingredients
100g (3½oz) unsalted butter, plus extra for greasing
100g (3½oz) soft light brown sugar
75g (2½oz) dried cranberries, roughly chopped
50g (1¾oz) pecans, roughly chopped
finely grated zest of 2 oranges and juice of 1 orange
2 eggs
125ml (4fl oz) milk
225g (8oz) self-raising flour
½ tsp baking powder
½ tsp cinnamon
100g (3½oz) icing sugar, sifted

Method
1 Preheat the oven to 180°C (350°F/Gas 4). Grease the tin and line with parchment. In a pan, melt the butter. Leave to cool slightly, then stir in the sugar, cranberries, pecans, and zest of 1 orange. Whisk together the eggs and milk, then stir them in as well.

2 In a separate bowl, sift together the flour, baking powder, and cinnamon. Fold into the batter, mixing well. Tip into the tin. Bake in the centre of the oven for 50–60 minutes. Leave to cool slightly, then turn out.

3 Mix the icing sugar and remaining zest. Add enough orange juice for a drizzling consistency. Drizzle the frosting over the cooled cake and leave to dry before slicing.

STORE Will keep in a container for 3 days.

Sweet Potato Bread

Savoury sounding, this is very much a sweet cake and similar to a banana bread in looks and texture.

| MAKES 1 LOAF | 10 MINS | 1 HOUR | UP TO 4 WEEKS |

Special equipment
900g (2lb) loaf tin

Ingredients
100g (3½oz) unsalted butter, softened, plus extra for greasing
175g (6oz) sweet potatoes, peeled and diced
200g (7oz) plain flour
2 tsp baking powder
pinch of salt
½ tsp mixed spice
½ tsp cinnamon
125g (4½oz) caster sugar
50g (1¾oz) pecans, roughly chopped
50g (1¾oz) chopped dates
100ml (3½fl oz) sunflower oil
2 eggs

Method
1 Grease and line the tin with parchment. Place the sweet potato in a pan, cover with water, and bring to a boil, then simmer for about 10 minutes until tender. Mash and set aside to cool.

2 Preheat the oven to 170°C (335°F/Gas 3½). In a large bowl, sift together the flour, baking powder, salt, spices, and sugar. Add the pecans and dates and mix in thoroughly. Make a well in the centre.

3 In a jug, whisk the eggs with the oil until emulsified. Add the potato and stir until smooth. Pour into the flour mix and stir together until well combined and smooth.

4 Pour the batter into the tin and smooth the top with a palette knife. Bake in the centre of the oven for 1 hour until well risen and a skewer comes out clean. Leave to cool for 5 minutes before turning out.

STORE The cake will keep in an airtight container for 3 days.

celebration cakes

Rich Fruit Cake

This recipe makes a wonderfully moist, rich fruit cake, ideal for Christmas, weddings, christenings, or birthdays.

SERVES 16 **25 MINS** **2½ HOURS**

Soaking time
overnight

Special equipment
20–25cm (8–10in) deep round
  cake tin

Ingredients
200g (7oz) sultanas
400g (14oz) raisins
350g (12oz) prunes, chopped
350g (12oz) glacé cherries

2 small dessert apples, peeled,
  cored, and diced
600ml (1 pint) cider
4 tsp mixed spice
200g (7oz) unsalted butter, softened
175g (6oz) dark brown sugar
3 eggs, beaten
150g (5½oz) ground almonds
280g (10oz) plain flour

2 tsp baking powder
400g (14oz) ready-made marzipan
2–3 tbsp apricot jam
3 large egg whites
500g (1lb 2oz) icing sugar

1 Place the sultanas, raisins, prunes, cherries, apple, cider, and spice in a saucepan.

2 Simmer over medium-low heat and cover for 20 minutes until most of the liquid is absorbed.

3 Remove from the heat. Leave overnight at room temperature; the fruits will absorb liquid.

4 Preheat the oven to 160°C (325°F/Gas 3). Double-line the tin with baking parchment.

5 With an electric whisk, cream the butter and sugar in a large bowl until fluffy.

6 Add the eggs, a little at a time, beating very well after each addition to avoid curdling.

7 Gently fold in the fruit mix and ground almonds, trying to keep volume in the batter.

8 Sift the flour and baking powder into the bowl, and gently fold into the mixture.

9 Spoon the batter into the prepared tin, cover with foil, and bake for 2½ hours.

CELEBRATION CAKES

10 Test the cake is ready: a skewer inserted into the centre should come out clean.

11 Leave to cool, then turn out onto a wire rack to cool completely. Remove the parchment.

12 Trim the cake to level it. Transfer to a stand and hold in place with some marzipan.

13 Warm the jam and brush thickly over the whole cake. This will help the marzipan stick.

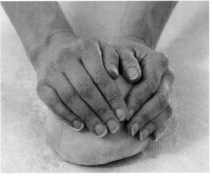

14 On a lightly floured surface, knead the remaining marzipan until softened.

15 Roll out the softened marzipan until wide enough to cover the cake.

16 Drape the marzipan over the rolling pin and lift it over the cake.

17 With your hands, gently ease the marzipan into place, smoothing out any bumps.

18 With a small sharp knife, cut away any excess marzipan from the base of the cake.

19 Place the egg whites in a bowl and sift in the icing sugar, stirring well to combine.

20 With an electric whisk, beat the icing sugar mixture for 10 minutes until stiff.

21 Spread the icing with a palette knife.
PREPARE AHEAD Will keep, un-iced, for 8 weeks.

Fruit Cake variations

Prune Chocolate Dessert Cake

Soaked prunes give this rich, dark cake a warming depth of flavour, making it a perfect dessert for the winter months.

SERVES 8–10	30 MINS	40–45 MINS	UP TO 8 WEEKS

Soaking time
overnight

Special equipment
22cm (9in) round springform cake tin

Ingredients
100g (3½oz) ready-to-eat prunes, chopped
100ml (3½fl oz) brandy or cold black tea
125g (4½oz) unsalted butter,
  plus extra for greasing
250g (9oz) good-quality dark chocolate,
  broken into pieces
3 eggs, separated
150g (5½oz) caster sugar
100g (3½oz) ground almonds
cocoa powder, sifted, for dusting
double cream, whipped, to serve (optional)

Method

1 Soak the prunes in the brandy or tea overnight. When ready to bake, preheat the oven to 180°C (350°F/Gas 4). Grease the tin and line the base with baking parchment.

2 Gently melt the chocolate and butter in a heatproof bowl over a pan of simmering water, and then cool. Beat the egg yolks and sugar together with an electric whisk. Whisk the egg whites separately into soft peaks.

3 Mix the cooled chocolate into the egg yolk mixture. Fold in the ground almonds, prunes, and soaking liquid, mixing till well combined. Beat 2 tablespoons of the egg white into the batter to loosen the mixture slightly. Gently fold in the remaining egg white.

4 Pour the mixture into the tin and bake for 40–45 minutes until the surface is springy; the centre will be slightly soft. Leave the cake to cool in its tin for a while, then turn it out onto a wire rack to cool. Remove the parchment.

5 Serve the cake upside down, as this will give a smoother finish to the top. Dust with cocoa powder and serve with the cream.

PREPARE AHEAD This will keep in an airtight container for up to 5 days.

Tea Bread

A simple recipe; don't forget to use the soaking water as well as the fruit.

SERVES 8–10	20 MINS	1 HOUR	UP TO 4 WEEKS

Soaking time
overnight

Special equipment
900g (2lb) loaf tin

Ingredients
250g (9oz) mixed dried fruit (sultanas, raisins,
  currants, and mixed peel)
100g (3½oz) soft light brown sugar
250ml (8fl oz) cold black tea
unsalted butter, for greasing
50g (1¾oz) walnuts or hazelnuts, roughly chopped
1 egg, beaten
200g (7oz) self-raising flour

Method

1 Mix the dried fruit and sugar together, and leave to soak in the cold tea overnight. When ready to bake, preheat the oven to 180°C (350°F/Gas 4). Grease the loaf tin and line the base with baking parchment.

2 Add the nuts and the egg to the soaked fruit, and mix well to combine. Sift over the flour, and fold it in, mixing thoroughly.

3 Bake in the centre of the oven for 1 hour or until the top is dark golden brown and springy to the touch.

4 Leave to cool slightly in its tin, then turn out onto a wire rack to cool completely. Remove the baking parchment. This is best served sliced or toasted with butter.

STORE The bread will keep in an airtight container for 5 days.

Light Fruit Cake

Not everyone enjoys a classic rich fruit cake, especially after a hearty celebration meal. This lighter version is a quick and easy alternative that's less heavy on the fruit.

SERVES 8–12	25 MINS	1¾ HOURS	UP TO 8 WEEKS

Special equipment
20cm (8in) deep round cake tin

Ingredients
175g (6oz) unsalted butter, softened
175g (6oz) light soft brown sugar
3 large eggs
250g (9oz) self-raising flour, sifted
2–3 tbsp milk
300g (10½oz) mixed dried fruit (sultanas, raisins, glacé cherries, and mixed peel)

Method

1 Preheat the oven to 180°C (350°F/Gas 4). Line the tin with baking parchment.

2 In a bowl, beat the butter and sugar together with an electric hand whisk until pale and creamy. Then beat in the eggs, one at a time, adding a little of the flour after each one. Fold in the remaining flour and the milk. Add the dried fruit and fold in until well combined.

3 Spoon the mixture into the tin, level the top, and bake for 1½–1¾ hours until firm to the touch and a skewer inserted into the middle of the cake comes out clean. Leave in the tin to cool completely. Remove the baking parchment.

STORE The cake will keep in an airtight container for 3 days.

Plum Pudding

So-named because it contains prunes, this is a classic Christmas dish, here using butter instead of the traditional beef suet.

SERVES 8–10 **45 MINS** **8–10 HOURS** **UP TO 1 YEAR**

Soaking time
overnight

Special equipment
1kg (2¼lb) pudding bowl

Ingredients
85g (3oz) raisins
60g (2oz) currants
100g (3½oz) sultanas
45g (1½oz) mixed peel, chopped
115g (4oz) mixed dried fruit,
 such as figs, dates, and cherries
150ml (5fl oz) beer
1 tbsp whisky or brandy
finely grated zest and juice of 1 orange
finely grated zest and juice of 1 lemon
85g (3oz) ready-to-eat prunes, chopped
150ml (5fl oz) cold black tea
1 dessert apple, peeled, cored, and grated
115g (4oz) unsalted butter, melted,
 plus extra for greasing
175g (6oz) dark soft brown sugar
1 tbsp black treacle
2 eggs, beaten
60g (2oz) self-raising flour
1 tsp mixed spice
115g (4oz) fresh white breadcrumbs
60g (2oz) chopped almonds
brandy butter, cream, or custard,
 to serve (optional)

Method

1 Place the first 9 ingredients into a large bowl and mix well. Put the prunes in a small bowl and pour in the tea. Cover the bowls and leave to soak overnight.

2 Drain the prunes and discard any remaining tea. Add the prunes and the apple to the rest of the fruit, followed by the butter, sugar, treacle, and eggs, stirring well.

3 Sift in the flour along with the mixed spice, then stir in the breadcrumbs and almonds. Mix until all the ingredients are well combined.

4 Grease the pudding bowl and pour in the mixture. Cover the top of the bowl with 2 layers of baking parchment and 1 layer of foil. Tie the layers to the bowl with string, then put the bowl into a pan of simmering water that comes at least halfway up the side of the bowl. Steam for 8–10 hours.

5 Check regularly to make sure that the water level does not drop too low. Serve with brandy butter, cream, or custard.

PREPARE AHEAD If well sealed, the pudding will keep for up to 1 year in a cool place.

BAKER'S TIP
When steaming a pudding for an extended time, it is very important that the water level in the pan should not drop too low. There are a couple of easy ways to avoid this. Either set a timer every hour, to remind you to check the water level, or put a marble in the pan so it rattles when the water level drops.

Stollen

This rich, fruity sweet bread, originally from Germany, is traditionally served at Christmas and makes a great alternative to Christmas cake or mince pies.

| SERVES 12 | 30 MINS | 50 MINS | UP TO 4 WEEKS |

Soaking time
overnight

Rising and proving time
2–3 hours

Ingredients
200g (7oz) raisins
100g (3½oz) currants
100ml (3½fl oz) rum

400g (14oz) strong white bread flour, plus extra for dusting
2 tsp dried yeast
60g (2oz) caster sugar
100ml (3½fl oz) milk
½ tsp vanilla extract
pinch of salt
½ tsp mixed spice
2 large eggs
175g (6oz) unsalted butter, softened and diced
200g (7oz) mixed peel
100g (3½oz) ground almonds
icing sugar, for dusting

Method

1 Put the raisins and currants into a large bowl, pour over the rum, and leave to soak overnight.

2 The following day, sift the flour into a large bowl. Make a well in the centre, sprinkle in the yeast, and add a teaspoon of sugar. Gently heat the milk until lukewarm and pour on top of the yeast. Leave to stand at room temperature for 15 minutes or until it turns frothy.

3 Add the rest of the sugar, vanilla extract, salt, mixed spice, eggs, and butter. Mix everything together with a wooden spoon and then knead the dough for 5 minutes until smooth.

4 Transfer to a lightly floured surface. Add the mixed peel, raisins and currants, and almonds, kneading for a few minutes until mixed. Return the dough to the bowl, cover loosely with cling film, and leave to rise in a warm place for 1–1½ hours until doubled.

5 Preheat the oven to 160°C (325°F/Gas 3). Line a baking tray with baking parchment. On a floured surface, roll out the dough to make a 30 x 25cm (12 x 10in) rectangle. Fold one long side over, just beyond the middle, then fold over the other long side to overlap the first, curving it slightly on top to create the stollen shape. Transfer to the baking tray and put in a warm place for 1–1½ hours to prove until doubled in size.

6 Bake in the oven for 50 minutes or until risen and pale golden. Check after 30–35 minutes and if browning too much, cover loosely with foil. Transfer to a wire rack to cool completely, then generously dust with icing sugar.

STORE The stollen will keep in an airtight container for 4 days.

BAKER'S TIP
Stollen can be made with any combination of dried fruits. It can be plain as in this recipe, or stuffed with a marzipan or frangipane layer. Any leftovers are great for breakfast, lightly toasted, with butter.

Chocolate Chestnut Roulade

Perfect for a winter celebration, this rolled sponge is filled with a rich chestnut purée mixed with whipped cream.

SERVES 8–10 **50–55 MINS** **5–7 MINS** **8 WEEKS, UNFILLED**

Special equipment
30 x 37cm (12 x 15in) Swiss roll tin
piping bag and star nozzle

Ingredients
butter, for greasing
35g (1¼oz) cocoa powder
1 tbsp plain flour
pinch of salt
5 eggs, separated
150g (5½oz) caster sugar

For the filling
125g (4½oz) chestnut purée
2 tbsp dark rum
175ml (6fl oz) double cream
30g (1oz) good-quality dark
  chocolate, broken into pieces
caster sugar to taste (optional)

For decoration
50g (1¾oz) caster sugar
2 tbsp dark rum
125ml (4fl oz) double cream
dark chocolate, grated with
  a vegetable peeler,
  to produce shavings

1 Preheat the oven to 220°C (425°F/Gas 7). Grease a baking sheet. Line with parchment.

2 Sift the cocoa powder, flour, and salt into a large bowl and set aside.

3 Beat the egg yolks with two-thirds of the sugar; it should leave a ribbon trail.

4 Whisk the egg whites until stiff. Sprinkle in the remaining sugar and whisk again until glossy.

5 Sift one-third of the cocoa mixture over the yolk mixture. Add one-third of the egg whites.

6 Fold together lightly. Add the remaining cocoa mixture and egg white in 2 batches.

7 Pour the batter onto the prepared baking sheet. Spread the batter almost to the edges.

8 Bake in the bottom of the oven for 5–7 minutes. The cake will be risen and just firm.

9 Remove the cake from the oven, invert onto a damp tea towel and peel off the parchment.

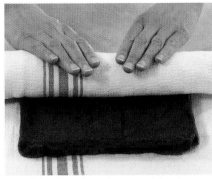

10 Tightly roll up the cake around the damp tea towel and leave to cool.

11 Put the chestnut purée in a bowl with the rum. Whip the cream until it forms soft peaks.

12 Melt the chocolate in a bowl over a pan of simmering water. Stir into the chestnut mixture.

13 Fold the chocolate and chestnut mixture into the whipped cream. Add sugar to taste.

14 Simmer 50g (1¾oz) in 4 tablespoons of water for 1 minute. Cool and stir in rum.

15 Unroll the cake on fresh parchment. Brush with syrup and spread the chestnut mix.

16 Using the parchment underneath, carefully roll up the filled cake as tightly as possible.

17 Whip the cream and remaining sugar until stiff. Fill the piping bag with the cream.

18 Trim the edges with a serrated knife. Transfer the roulade to a serving plate. Decorate with the whipped cream and chocolate shavings. The roulade is best eaten on the day.

Chocolate Roulade variations

Chocolate Log

The Christmas classic, pairing dark chocolate with raspberry.

SERVES 10	30 MINS	15 MINS	UP TO 24 WEEKS

Special equipment
20 x 28cm (8 x 11in) Swiss roll tin

Ingredients
3 eggs
85g (3oz) caster sugar
85g (3oz) plain flour
3 tbsp cocoa powder
½ tsp baking powder
icing sugar, for dusting
200ml (7fl oz) double cream
140g (5oz) dark chocolate, chopped
3 tbsp raspberry jam

Method

1 Preheat the oven to 180°C (350°F/Gas 4). Line the Swiss roll tin with parchment.

2 Whisk the eggs with the sugar and a tablespoon of water for 5 minutes or until pale and light. Sift the flour, cocoa powder, and baking powder into the beaten eggs, then carefully and quickly fold in.

3 Pour the mixture into the tin, and bake for 12 minutes until springy to the touch. Turn it out onto a piece of baking parchment. Peel the paper from the base of the cake and discard. Roll the sponge up around the fresh parchment. Leave to cool.

4 To make the icing, pour the cream into a small pan, bring to a boil, then remove from the heat. Add the chopped chocolate and leave it to melt, stirring occasionally. Allow the mixture to cool and thicken.

5 Unroll the cake and spread raspberry jam over the surface. Spread one-third of the icing on the jam and roll it. Place the cake seam-side down. Spread the rest of the icing all over the cake. Use a fork to create ridges down the length and ends of the cake. Transfer to a serving plate and dust with icing sugar.

STORE The cake will keep, chilled, for 2 days.

Chocolate Amaretti Roulade

Crushed Amaretti biscuits add texture and crunch to this beautiful and indulgent roulade. ▶

SERVES 6–8	25–30 MINS	20 MINS	8 WEEKS, UNFILLED

Special equipment
20 x 28cm (8 x 11in) Swiss roll tin

Ingredients
6 large eggs, separated
150g (5½oz) caster sugar
50g (1¾oz) cocoa powder, plus extra for dusting
icing sugar, for dusting
300ml (10fl oz) double cream or whipping cream
2–3 tbsp Amaretto or brandy
20 Amaretti biscuits, crushed, plus 2 for topping
50g (1¾oz) dark chocolate

Method

1 Preheat the oven to 180°C (350°F/Gas 4). Line the tin with parchment. Put the egg yolks and sugar in a bowl set over a pan of simmering water and beat with an electric whisk for 10 minutes until creamy. Remove from the heat. In another bowl, beat the egg whites with a clean whisk till soft peaks form.

2 Sift the cocoa powder into the egg yolk mixture and gently fold in, along with the egg whites. Pour into the tin and smooth into the corners. Bake for 20 minutes or until just firm to the touch. Cool slightly before carefully turning the cake out, face down, onto a sheet of baking parchment well dusted with icing sugar. Cool for 30 minutes.

3 Whisk the cream with an electric whisk until soft peaks form. Trim the sides of the cake to neaten them, then drizzle over the Amaretto or brandy. Spread with the cream, scatter with the crushed Amaretti biscuits, then grate over most of the chocolate.

4 Starting from one of the short sides, roll the roulade up, using the parchment to help keep it tightly together. Place on a serving plate with the seam underneath. Crumble over the extra biscuits, grate over the remaining chocolate, and dust with a little icing sugar and cocoa powder. The roulade is best eaten on the same day.

Chocolate and Buttercream Roll

This chocolatey variation on a Swiss roll is simple to make and always a hit with kids – perfect for a children's party.

SERVES 8–10	20–25 MINS	10 MINS

Special equipment
20 x 28cm (8 x 11in) Swiss roll tin

Ingredients
3 large eggs
75g (2½oz) caster sugar
50g (1¾oz) plain flour
25g (scant 1oz) cocoa powder, plus extra for dusting
75g (2½oz) butter, softened
125g (4½oz) icing sugar

Method

1 Preheat the oven to 200°C (400°F/Gas 6) and line the tin with parchment. Set a bowl over a pan of simmering water, add the eggs and sugar, and whisk for 5–10 minutes until thick and creamy. Remove from the heat, sift in the flour and cocoa, and fold in.

2 Pour the mixture into the tin and bake for 10 minutes or until springy to the touch. Cover with a damp tea towel and cool. Turn the sponge out, face down, onto a sheet of parchment dusted with cocoa powder. Peel off the parchment it was baked on.

3 Whisk the butter until creamy. Beat in the icing sugar, a little at a time, then spread the mixture over the sponge. Using the parchment to help you, roll the sponge up.

STORE The cake will keep, chilled, for 3 days.

Black Forest Gâteau

Newly resurrected to its glorious best, this classic German cake deserves its place on a celebration table.

SERVES 8	55 MINS	40 MINS	UP TO 4 WEEKS

Special equipment
23cm (9in) round springform cake tin
piping bag and star nozzle

Ingredients
85g (3oz) butter, melted,
  plus extra for greasing
6 eggs
175g (6oz) golden caster sugar
125g (4½oz) plain flour
50g (1¾oz) cocoa powder
1 tsp vanilla extract

For the filling and decoration
2 x 425g cans pitted black cherries,
  drained, 6 tbsp juice reserved, and
  cherries from 1 can roughly chopped
4 tbsp Kirsch
600ml (1 pint) double cream
150g (5½oz) dark chocolate, grated

1 Preheat the oven to 180°C (350°F/Gas 4). Grease and line the tin with baking parchment.

2 Put the eggs and sugar into a large heatproof bowl that will fit over a saucepan.

3 Place the bowl over a pan of simmering water. Don't let the bowl touch the water.

4 Whisk until the mixture is pale and thick, and will hold a trail from the beaters.

5 Remove from the heat and whisk for another 5 minutes or until cooled slightly.

6 Sift the flour and cocoa together, and gently fold into the egg mixture using a spatula.

7 Fold in the vanilla and butter. Transfer to the prepared tin and level the surface.

8 Bake in the oven for 40 minutes or until risen and just shrinking away from the sides.

9 Turn out onto a wire rack, discard the paper, and cover with a clean cloth. Let it cool.

CELEBRATION CAKES

10 Carefully cut the cake into 3 layers. Use a serrated knife and long sweeping strokes.

11 Combine the reserved cherry juice with the Kirsch, and drizzle a third over each layer.

12 Whip the cream in a separate bowl until it just holds shape; it should not be too stiff.

13 Place a layer of cake on a plate. Spread with cream and half the chopped cherries.

14 Repeat with the second sponge. Top with the final sponge, baked side up. Press down.

15 Cover the side with a layer of cream. Put the remaining cream in the piping bag.

16 Press grated chocolate onto the creamy sides with a palette knife.

17 Pipe a ring of cream swirls around the cake and place the whole cherries inside.

18 Sprinkle any remaining chocolate evenly over the peaks of piped cream, to serve.
PREPARE AHEAD The cake can be covered and chilled for up to 3 days.

Gâteau variations

German Cream Cheese Torte

This German dessert is a cross between a cheesecake and a sponge cake. It makes a good party dessert as it can be prepared well in advance.

SERVES **40** **30**
8–10 **MINS** **MINS**

Chilling time
3 hrs, or overnight

Special equipment
22cm (9in) round springform cake tin

Ingredients
150g (5½oz) unsalted butter, softened,
   or soft margarine, plus extra for greasing
225g (8oz) caster sugar
3 eggs
150g (5½oz) self-raising flour
1 tsp baking powder
juice and finely grated zest of 2 lemons,
   plus 1 extra lemon for zesting to decorate
5 sheets of gelatine (8.5g/¼oz)
250ml (8fl oz) double cream
250g (9oz) quark, or see Baker's Tip
icing sugar, for dusting

Method

1 Preheat the oven to 180°C (350°F/Gas 4). Grease the tin and line with parchment.

2 Cream together the butter or margarine and 150g (5½oz) sugar. Beat in the eggs, one at a time, until smooth and creamy. Sift together the flour and baking powder, and fold into the batter with half the zest. Spoon into the tin and bake for 30 minutes or until well risen. Turn the cake out onto a wire rack. Slice it in half horizontally with a serrated knife. Leave to cool completely.

3 For the filling, put the gelatine in a bowl of cold water for a few minutes until it is soft and pliable. Heat the lemon juice in a pan, then remove from the heat. Squeeze out any excess water from the gelatine and add to the lemon juice. Stir until dissolved, and cool.

4 Whisk the cream until firm. Beat together the quark and remaining zest and sugar. Beat in the lemon juice. Fold in the cream.

5 Spoon the filling onto a cake half. Slice the second half into 8 pieces and arrange on top of the filling; pre-cutting the top layer makes it easier to serve. Chill for at least 3 hours or overnight. Sift over icing sugar and sprinkle with the extra lemon zest.

PREPARE AHEAD Can be made up to 3 days ahead and kept in the refrigerator.

BAKER'S TIP
If you cannot find any quark it can easily be substituted with low-fat cottage cheese, processed to a paste in a food processor with blade attachment.

Bavarian Raspberry Gâteau

When raspberries are not in season, you can use frozen berries.

SERVES	55–60	20–25
8	MINS	MINS

Chilling time
4 hrs

Special equipment
22cm (9in) round springform cake tin
blender

Ingredients
60g (2oz) unsalted butter, plus extra for greasing
125g (4½oz) plain flour, plus extra for dusting
pinch of salt
4 eggs, beaten
135g (5oz) caster sugar
2 tbsp Kirsch

For the raspberry cream
500g (1lb 2oz) raspberries
3 tbsp Kirsch
200g (7oz) caster sugar
250ml (8fl oz) double cream
1 litre (1¾ pints) milk
1 vanilla pod, split, or 2 tsp vanilla extract
10 egg yolks
3 tbsp cornflour
10g (¼oz) powdered gelatine

Method

1 Preheat the oven to 220°C (425°F/Gas 7). Grease the tin with butter and line the base with buttered parchment. Sprinkle in 2–3 tablespoons flour. Melt the butter and let it cool. Sift the flour and salt into a bowl. Put the eggs in a separate bowl and beat in the sugar, using an electric whisk, for 5 minutes.

2 Sift one-third of the flour mixture over the egg mixture and fold in. Add the remaining flour in 2 batches. Pour in the butter and fold in. Pour into the tin and bake for 20–25 minutes until the cake has risen.

3 Turn out the cake onto a wire rack. Let cool. Remove the parchment. Trim the top and bottom so that they are flat. Cut the cake horizontally in half. Clean, dry, and re-grease the tin. Put a cake round in the tin and sprinkle it with 1 tablespoon of Kirsch.

4 Purée three-quarters of the berries in a blender, then work through a sieve to remove the pips. Stir in 1 tablespoon of Kirsch with 100g (3½oz) of the sugar. Whip the cream until it forms soft peaks.

5 Put the milk in a pan. Add the vanilla pod (if using). Bring to a boil. Remove the pan from the heat, cover, and let stand in a warm place for 10–15 minutes. Remove the pod. Set aside one-quarter of the milk. Stir the remaining sugar into the milk in the pan.

6 Beat the egg yolks and cornflour in a bowl. Add the hot milk and whisk until smooth. Pour the yolk mixture back into the pan and cook over medium heat, stirring, just until the custard comes to a boil. Stir in the reserved milk and the vanilla extract (if using).

7 Strain the custard equally into 2 bowls. Let cool. Stir 2 tablespoons of Kirsch into 1 bowl. Set this custard aside to serve with the finished dessert. Sprinkle the powdered gelatine over 4 tablespoons of water in a small pan and let soften for 5 minutes.

Heat until the gelatine is melted and pourable. Stir into the bowl of unflavoured custard, along with the raspberry purée.

8 Set the bowl in a pan of iced water. Stir the mixture until it thickens. Remove the bowl from the water. Fold the raspberry custard into the whipped cream. Pour half into the cake tin. Sprinkle a few reserved whole raspberries. Pour the remaining Bavarian cream on the berries. Sprinkle 1 tablespoon of Kirsch over the second cake round.

9 Lightly press the cake round, sprinkled-side down, on the cream. Cover with cling film and refrigerate for at least 4 hours until firm. To serve, remove the side of the tin and place on a serving plate. Decorate the top of the cake with the reserved raspberries, and serve the Kirsch custard sauce separately.

PREPARE AHEAD The gâteau can be made up to 2 days ahead and kept in the refrigerator; remove 1 hour before serving.

Bienenstich

The name of this German recipe translates as "bee sting cake". Legend has it that the honey attracts bees who sting the baker!

SERVES 8–10 | **20 MINS** | **20–25 MINS**

Rising and proving time
1 hr 5 mins–1 hr 20 mins

Special equipment
20cm (8in) round cake tin

Ingredients
140g (5oz) plain flour, plus extra for dusting
15g (½oz) unsalted butter, softened and diced, plus extra for greasing
½ tbsp caster sugar
1½ tsp dried yeast
pinch of salt
1 egg
oil, for greasing

For the glaze
30g (1oz) butter
20g (¾oz) caster sugar
1 tbsp clear honey
1 tbsp double cream
30g (1oz) flaked almonds
1 tsp lemon juice

For the crème pâtissière
250ml (8fl oz) full-fat milk
25g (scant 1oz) cornflour
2 vanilla pods, split lengthways, deseeded, pods and seeds retained
60g (2oz) caster sugar
3 egg yolks
25g (scant 1oz) unsalted butter, diced

Method

1 Sift the flour into a bowl. Quickly rub in the butter, then add the sugar, yeast, and salt, and mix well. Beat in the egg and add just enough water to make a soft dough.

2 Knead on a floured surface for 5–10 minutes or until smooth, elastic, and shiny. Put in a clean, oiled bowl, cover with cling film, and leave to rise in a warm place for 45–60 minutes or until doubled in size.

3 Grease the cake tin and line the base with baking parchment. Knock back the dough and roll it out into a circle to fit the tin. Push it into the tin and cover with cling film. Leave to prove for 20 minutes.

4 To make the glaze, melt the butter in a small pan, then add the sugar, honey, and cream. Cook over low heat until the sugar has dissolved, then increase the heat and bring to a boil. Allow to simmer for 3 minutes, then remove the pan from the heat, and add the almonds and lemon juice. Allow to cool.

5 Preheat the oven to 190°C (375°F/Gas 5). Carefully spread the glaze over the dough, leave to rise for another 10 minutes, then bake for 20–25 minutes; if it starts to brown too quickly, cover loosely with foil. Allow to cool in the tin for 30 minutes, then transfer to a wire rack.

6 Meanwhile, make the crème pâtissière. Pour the milk into a heavy saucepan and add the cornflour, vanilla seeds and pods, and half the sugar. Place over low heat. Whisk the egg yolks with the remaining sugar in a bowl. Continue whisking and slowly pour in the hot milk. Transfer to the pan and whisk until it just comes to a boil, then remove from the heat.

7 Immediately place the whole saucepan into a bowl of iced water and remove the vanilla pods. Once the sauce has cooled, add the butter, and briskly whisk into the sauce until it is smooth and glossy.

8 Slice the cake in half. Spread a thick layer of crème pâtissière on the bottom half, then place the almond layer on top. Transfer to a serving plate.

BAKER'S TIP

This German classic is traditionally filled with crème pâtissière, as in this recipe. It makes a smooth, luxurious filling which these days is a real treat. However, if you are pushed for time, an easier option would be to fill the cake with whipped double cream, lightly scented with ½ teaspoon vanilla extract.

Kugelhopf

Dark raisins and chopped almonds are baked into this classic kugelhopf, an Alsatian favourite. A dusting of icing sugar hints at the sweet filling.

| MAKES 1 RING | 45–50 MINS | 45–50 MINS | UP TO 8 WEEKS |

Rising and proving time
2–2½ hrs

Special equipment
1-litre (1¾-pint) ring mould

Ingredients
150ml (5fl oz) milk
2 tbsp granulated sugar
150g (5½oz) unsalted butter, diced,

plus extra for greasing
1 tbsp dried yeast
500g (1lb 2oz) strong white bread flour
1 tsp salt
3 eggs, beaten
90g (3oz) raisins
60g (2oz) blanched almonds, chopped,
  plus 7 whole blanched almonds
icing sugar, for dusting

Method

1 Bring the milk to the boil in a saucepan. Add 4 tablespoons to a bowl and leave to cool till it is lukewarm. Add the sugar and butter to the remaining milk in the pan, and stir until melted. Allow it to cool.

2 Sprinkle the yeast over the milk in the bowl and let stand for 5 minutes until dissolved, stirring once. Sift the flour and salt into a bowl and add the dissolved yeast, eggs, and the milk mixture from the pan.

3 Gradually draw in the flour and work it into the other ingredients to form a smooth dough. Knead for 5–7 minutes, until very elastic and sticky. Cover with a damp tea towel and let rise in a warm place for 1–1½ hours or until doubled .

4 Meanwhile, grease the mould with butter. Freeze the mould until the butter is hard (about 10 minutes), then butter it again. Pour boiling water over the raisins and allow them to plump up.

5 Knock back the dough lightly with your hand to push out the air. Drain the raisins, reserving 7 of them, and knead the rest into the dough with the chopped almonds. Arrange the reserved raisins and whole almonds at the bottom of the mould.

6 Shape the dough into the mould, cover with a tea towel, and leave to prove in a warm place for 30–40 minutes until it comes just above the top of the mould. Preheat the oven to 190°C (375°F/Gas 5).

7 Bake the kugelhopf until puffed and brown, and the bread starts to shrink from the side of the mould. It should take 45–50 minutes. Let it cool slightly. Turn out onto a wire rack and let cool completely. Just before serving, dust with icing sugar.

STORE The kugelhopf will keep in an airtight container for 3 days.

BAKER'S TIP

The dough of kugelhopf is very sticky. It is natural to want to add more flour, in order to make it look more like conventional dough. However, resist the temptation, as it would make the kugelhopf tough.

Chestnut Millefeuilles

Sure to impress, this dessert is actually quite easy to make and can be prepared up to 6 hours ahead and chilled.

SERVES 8 | 2 HOURS | 20–25 MINUTES

Chilling time
1 hr

Ingredients
375ml (13fl oz) milk
4 egg yolks
60g (2oz) granulated sugar
3 tbsp plain flour, sifted
2 tbsp dark rum

600g (1lb 5oz) puff pastry,
  shop-bought
250ml (8fl oz) double cream
500g (1lb 2oz) marrons glacés,
  coarsely crumbled
45g (1½oz) icing sugar,
  plus extra if needed

1 Heat the milk in a pan over medium heat until it just comes to a boil. Take off heat.

2 Whisk the egg yolks and granulated sugar for 2–3 minutes until thick. Whisk in the flour.

3 Gradually whisk the milk into the egg mixture until smooth. Return to a clean pan.

4 Bring to a boil, whisking, until thickened. Reduce heat to low and whisk for 2 minutes.

5 If lumps form in the pastry cream, remove from the heat and whisk until smooth again.

6 Let cool, then stir in the rum. Transfer to a bowl, cover with cling film, and chill for 1 hour.

7 Preheat the oven to 200°C (400°F/Gas 6). Sprinkle a baking sheet evenly with cold water.

8 Roll out the pastry to a rectangle a little larger than the baking sheet, about 3mm (⅛in) thick.

9 Roll the dough around a rolling pin. Unroll it onto the baking sheet. Let the edges overhang.

CELEBRATION CAKES

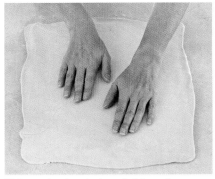

10 Press the dough down lightly on the baking sheet, then chill for about 15 minutes.

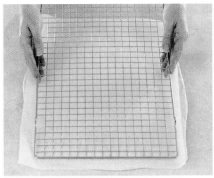

11 Prick the dough all over with a fork. Cover with parchment. Set a wire rack on top.

12 Bake for 15–20 minutes. Remove from the oven, grip the sheet and rack, invert the pastry.

13 Slide the baking sheet back under the pastry and bake for a further 10 minutes.

14 Remove from the oven and carefully slide the pastry onto a chopping board.

15 While still warm, trim round the edges with a large, sharp knife to neaten.

16 Cut the trimmed sheet lengthways into 3 equal strips. Allow to cool.

17 Pour the cream into a bowl and whip until fairly firm.

18 Using a large metal spoon, fold the whipped cream into the chilled pastry cream.

19 With a palette knife, spread half the cream mixture evenly over one pastry strip.

20 Sprinkle with half the chestnuts. Repeat to make 2 layers and top with the last strip.

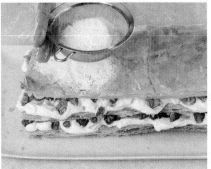

21 Sift over icing sugar and divide into portions with a serrated knife.

Millefeuilles variations

Chocolate Millefeuilles

Filled with dark chocolate cream and decorated with white chocolate drizzles, this version has wow factor in abundance.

| SERVES 8 | 2 HOURS | 25–30 MINS |

Chilling time
1 hr

Ingredients
1 quantity pastry cream, see page 88, steps 1–5
2 tbsp brandy
600g (1lb 5oz) puff pastry, shop-bought
375ml (13fl oz) double cream
50g (1¾oz) dark chocolate, melted and cooled
30g (1oz) white chocolate, melted and cooled

Method

1 Stir brandy into the cream, cover with cling film, and chill for 1 hour. Preheat the oven to 200°C (400°F/Gas 6).

2 Sprinkle a baking sheet with cold water. Roll out the pastry to a rectangle larger than the baking sheet. Transfer to the sheet, letting the edges overhang. Press the dough down. Chill for 15 minutes. Prick all over with a fork. Cover with parchment, then set a wire rack on top. Bake for 15–20 minutes until it just begins to brown. Gripping the sheet and rack, invert the pastry, slide the baking sheet back under and continue baking for 10 minutes until both sides are browned. Remove from the oven and slide the pastry onto a chopping board. Trim the edges while still warm, then cut lengthways into 3 equal strips. Let cool.

3 Whip the double cream until stiff. Stir it into the pastry cream with two-thirds of the melted dark chocolate. Cover and chill. Spread the remaining melted chocolate over one of the pastry strips to cover it. Let it set.

4 Put another pastry strip on a plate, spread with half the cream, top with the remaining strip, and spread with the rest of the cream. Cover with the chocolate-coated strip.

5 Put the white chocolate into one corner of a plastic bag. Twist the bag to enclose the chocolate and snip off the tip of the corner. Pipe trails of chocolate over the millefeuilles.

PREPARE AHEAD The dish can be made ahead and chilled for up to 6 hours.

Vanilla Slices

Classic pastries sandwiched with thick custard and sweet, luscious jam.

| MAKES 6 | 2 HOURS | 25–30 MINS |

Chilling time
1 hr

Special equipment
small piping bag with thin nozzle

Ingredients
250ml (13fl oz) double cream
1 quantity pastry cream, see page 88, steps 1–5
600g (1lb 5oz) puff pastry, shop-bought
100g (3½oz) icing sugar
1 tsp cocoa powder
½ jar smooth strawberry or raspberry jam

Method

1 Whip the double cream until stiff peaks form. Fold it into the pastry cream and chill. Preheat the oven to 200°C (400°F/Gas 6). Sprinkle a baking sheet with cold water. Roll out the pastry to a rectangle larger than the baking sheet and transfer to the sheet, letting the edges overhang. Press the dough down. Chill for 15 minutes.

2 Prick the dough with a fork. Cover with parchment, then set a wire rack on top. Bake for 15–20 minutes until it just begins to brown. Gripping the sheet and rack, invert the pastry. Slide the baking sheet back under and continue baking for 10 minutes until both sides are browned. Remove from the oven and slide the pastry on to a chopping board. While still warm, cut it into 5 x 10cm (2 x 4in) rectangles, in multiples of 3.

3 For the icing, mix the icing sugar with 1–1½ tablespoons cold water. Mix 2 tablespoons of the icing with the cocoa to make a small amount of chocolate icing. Place the chocolate icing in a piping bag with a thin nozzle. Take one-third of the pastry pieces and spread them with the white icing. While the icing is wet, pipe horizontal lines across it with the chocolate icing, then drag a skewer through the lines vertically to produce a striped effect. Allow to dry.

CELEBRATION CAKES

4 Spread the remaining pastry pieces with a thin layer of the jam. Spread a 1cm (½in) layer of pastry cream on top of the jam and tidy up the edges with a knife.

5 To assemble the vanilla slices, take a piece of pastry with jam and pastry cream, and place another gently on top. Press down lightly before topping with a third iced piece of pastry.

PREPARE AHEAD The dish can be made ahead and chilled for up to 6 hours.

Summer Fruit Millefeuilles

Beautiful and appetizing on a buffet table, or at a garden tea party. ▶

SERVES	2	25–30
8	HOURS	MINS

Chilling time
1 hr

Ingredients
1 quantity pastry cream, see page 88, steps 1–5
600g (1lb 5oz) puff pastry, shop-bought
250ml (8fl oz) double cream
400g (14oz) mixed summer fruits, such as strawberries, diced, and raspberries
icing sugar, for dusting

Method
1 Preheat the oven to 200°C (400°F/Gas 6). Sprinkle a baking sheet evenly with cold water. Roll out the pastry to a rectangle larger than the baking sheet, and about 3mm (⅛in) thick. Roll the dough around a rolling pin, then unroll it onto the baking sheet, letting the edges overhang. Press the dough down. Chill for about 15 minutes.

2 Prick the dough with a fork. Cover with parchment, then set a wire rack on top. Bake for 15–20 minutes until it just begins to brown. Gripping the sheet and rack, invert the pastry. Slide the baking sheet back under and continue baking for 10 minutes until both sides are browned.

Remove from the oven and slide the pastry onto a chopping board. While still warm, trim the edges, then cut lengthways into 3 equal strips. Allow to cool.

3 Whip the double cream until firm. Fold into the pastry cream. Spread half the pastry cream filling over 1 pastry strip. Sprinkle with half the fruit. Repeat with another pastry strip, to make 2 layers. Put the last pastry strip on top and press down gently. Sift the icing sugar thickly over the millefeuilles.

PREPARE AHEAD The dish can be made ahead and chilled for up to 6 hours.

BAKER'S TIP
Once you have mastered the art of assembling the pastry, millefeuilles can be made in endless variations: large, for an impressive buffet centrepiece, or in individual portions for an indulgent afternoon tea, sandwiched together with whatever filling you prefer.

small cakes

Vanilla Cream Cupcakes

Cupcakes are denser than fairy cakes, which enables them to carry more elaborate types of icing.

MAKES 24 | 20 MINS | 20–25 MINS | 4 WEEKS, UN-ICED

Special equipment
2 x 12-hole cupcake trays
piping bag and star nozzle (optional)

Ingredients
200g (7oz) plain flour, sifted
2 tsp baking powder
200g (7oz) caster sugar
½ tsp salt
100g (3½oz) unsalted butter, softened
3 eggs
150ml (5fl oz) milk
1 tsp vanilla extract

For the icing
200g (7oz) icing sugar
1 tsp vanilla extract
100g (3½oz) unsalted butter, softened
sugar sprinkles (optional)

1 Preheat the oven to 180°C (350°F/Gas 4). Place the first 5 ingredients in a bowl.

2 Mix together with your fingertips until it resembles fine breadcrumbs.

3 In another bowl, whisk the eggs, milk, and vanilla extract together until well blended.

4 Slowly pour the egg mixture into the dry ingredients, whisking all the time.

5 Whisk gently until smooth, being careful not to over-mix. Too much beating toughens cakes.

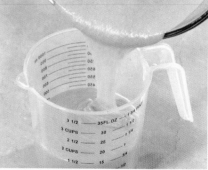

6 Pour all the cake batter into a jug to make it easier to handle.

7 Place the cupcake paper cases into the holes in the cupcake trays.

8 Carefully pour the cake mixture into the papers, filling each one only half full.

9 Bake in the preheated oven for 20–25 minutes until springy to the touch.

10 Test the cakes are done by inserting a skewer into the centre of one cupcake.

11 If traces of cake batter remain on the skewer, cook for a minute more, then test again.

12 Leave for a few minutes, then transfer the cupcakes to a wire rack to cool completely.

13 To make the icing, combine the icing sugar, vanilla extract, and butter in a bowl.

14 Beat with an electric whisk for 5 minutes until very light and fluffy.

15 Check the cakes have completely cooled, or they will melt the frosting.

16 If icing by hand, add a teaspoonful of the frosting mix to the top of each cake.

17 Then use the back of a spoon, dipped in warm water to smooth the surface.

To pipe the icing for a more professional finish, transfer the icing to the piping bag.

Pipe by squeezing out the icing with one hand, while holding the cake with the other.

Starting from the edge, pipe a spiral of icing that comes to a peak in the centre.

18 Decorate with sprinkles. **STORE** The cakes will keep in an airtight container for 3 days.

Cupcake variations

Chocolate Cupcakes

Classic chocolate cupcakes are another must-have recipe. A guaranteed winner at children's parties!

MAKES 24 | **20 MINS** | **20–25 MINS** | **4 WEEKS, UN-ICED**

Special equipment
2 x 12-hole cupcake trays
piping bag and star nozzle (optional)

Ingredients
200g (7oz) plain flour
2 tsp baking powder
4 tbsp cocoa powder
200g (7oz) caster sugar
½ tsp salt
100g (3½oz) unsalted butter, softened
3 eggs
150ml (5fl oz) milk
1 tsp vanilla extract
1 tbsp Greek yogurt

For the icing
100g (3½oz) unsalted butter, softened
175g (6oz) icing sugar
25g (scant 1oz) cocoa powder

Method
1 Preheat the oven to 180°C (350°F/Gas 4). Sift the flour, baking powder, and cocoa into a bowl. Add the sugar, salt, and butter. Mix until it resembles fine breadcrumbs. In a bowl, whisk the eggs, milk, vanilla extract, and yogurt together until well blended.

2 Slowly pour in the egg mixture to combine. Gently whisk until smooth. Place the cupcake cases into the trays. Carefully spoon the cake mixture into the cases, filling each one only half full.

3 Bake for 20–25 minutes until lightly coloured and springy to the touch. Leave for a few minutes, then transfer the cupcakes in their cases to a wire rack to cool completely.

4 For the icing, beat together the butter, icing sugar, and cocoa powder until smooth.

5 Ice by hand, using the back of a spoon dipped in warm water to smooth the surface, or transfer the icing to the piping bag and pipe onto the cakes.

STORE These cupcakes keep in an airtight container for 3 days.

Lemon Cupcakes

For a delicate taste, try flavouring the basic cupcake batter with lemon.

MAKES 24 | **20 MINS** | **20–25 MINS** | **4 WEEKS, UN-ICED**

Special equipment
2 x 12-hole cupcake trays
piping bag and star nozzle (optional)

Ingredients
200g (7oz) plain flour
2 tsp baking powder
200g (7oz) caster sugar
½ tsp salt
100g (3½oz) unsalted butter, softened
3 eggs
150ml (5fl oz) milk
finely grated zest and juice of 1 lemon

For the icing
200g (7oz) icing sugar
100g (3½oz) unsalted butter, softened

Method
1 Preheat the oven to 180°C (350°F/Gas 4). Sift the flour and baking powder into a bowl. Add the sugar, salt, and butter. Mix until it resembles fine breadcrumbs. In a bowl, whisk the eggs and milk until well blended.

2 Pour in the egg mixture to combine. Add half the lemon zest and all the lemon juice. Gently whisk until smooth. Place the cupcake paper cases into the cupcake trays. Spoon the mixture into the papers, filling each one only half full. Bake for 20–25 minutes until springy. Cool completely.

3 To make the icing, beat the icing sugar, butter, and remaining lemon zest until smooth. Ice by hand, with a teaspoon, or with the piping bag and star nozzle.

STORE These cupcakes keep in an airtight container for 3 days.

BAKER'S TIP
Due to their fairly dense texture, all these classic American cupcakes will keep well for a few days. If you prefer them well risen, replace the plain flour with self-raising flour but reduce the baking powder to 1 teaspoon, accordingly.

SMALL CAKES

Coffee and Walnut Cupcakes

Definitely one for adults, coffee and nuts add depth to these cupcakes.

MAKES 24 | 20 MINS | 20–25 MINS | 4 WEEKS, UN-ICED

Special equipment
2 x 12-hole cupcake trays
piping bag and star nozzle (optional)

Ingredients
200g (7oz) plain flour, plus extra for dusting
2 tsp baking powder
200g (7oz) caster sugar
½ tsp salt
100g (3½oz) unsalted butter, softened
3 eggs
150ml (5fl oz) milk
1 tbsp strong coffee powder mixed with 1 tbsp
   boiling water, and cooled, or 1 cooled espresso
100g (3½oz) halved walnuts, plus extra to decorate

For the icing
200g (7oz) icing sugar
100g (3½oz) unsalted butter, softened
1 tsp vanilla extract

Method

1 Preheat the oven to 180°C (350°F/Gas 4). Sift the flour and baking powder into a bowl. Add the sugar, salt, and butter. Mix until it resembles fine breadcrumbs. In a bowl, whisk the eggs and milk until well blended.

2 Pour in the egg mixture, add half the coffee, and whisk until smooth. Roughly chop the walnuts and toss them in a bowl with a little flour, then fold them into the batter. Place the cupcake cases in the trays. Spoon the mixture into the cases, filling each one only half full. Bake for 20–25 minutes until springy, then cool completely.

3 To make the icing, beat the icing sugar, butter, vanilla extract, and remaining coffee until smooth. Ice by hand, with a teaspoon, or with the piping bag and star nozzle. Top each cake with a walnut half.

STORE These cupcakes keep in an airtight container for 3 days.

Fondant Fancies

Dainty in size, gorgeous to look at, and delectable to eat, these little cakes are perfect for a party or as a special teatime treat.

MAKES 16 | 20–25 MINS | 25 MINS

Special equipment
20cm (8in) square cake tin

Ingredients
175g (6oz) unsalted butter, softened, plus extra for greasing
175g (6oz) caster sugar
3 large eggs
1 tsp vanilla extract
175g (6oz) self-raising flour, sifted
2 tbsp milk
2–3 tbsp raspberry or red cherry conserve

For the buttercream
75g (2½oz) unsalted butter, softened
150g (5½oz) icing sugar

For the icing
juice of ½ lemon
450g (1lb) icing sugar
1–2 drops natural pink food colouring
icing flowers, to decorate (optional)

Method

1 Preheat the oven to 190°C (375°F/Gas 5). Grease the cake tin and line the base with baking parchment. Place the butter and sugar in a large bowl and beat until pale and fluffy. Set aside.

2 Lightly beat the eggs and vanilla extract in another large bowl. Add about one-quarter of the egg mixture and a tablespoon of the flour to the butter mixture and beat well. Add the rest of the egg mixture, a little at a time, beating as you go. Add the remaining flour and the milk, and gently fold in.

3 Transfer the mixture to the prepared tin and bake in the middle of the oven for about 25 minutes or until lightly golden and springy to the touch. Remove from the oven, leave to cool in the tin for about 10 minutes, then remove from the tin and cool upside down on a wire rack. Remove the baking parchment.

4 To make the buttercream, beat the butter with the icing sugar until smooth. Set aside. Slice the cake horizontally with a serrated knife and spread the fruit conserve on one half and the buttercream on the other. Sandwich the layers together, then cut the cake into 16 equal squares.

5 To make the icing, put the lemon juice in a measuring jug and fill it up to 60ml (2fl oz) with hot water. Mix this with the icing sugar, stirring continuously and adding more hot water as required until the mixture is smooth. Add the pink food colouring and stir well.

6 Use a palette knife to transfer the cakes to a wire rack placed over a board or plate (to catch the drips). Drizzle with the icing to cover the cakes completely, or just cover the tops, and allow the icing to drip down the sides so the sponge layers are visible. Decorate with icing flowers (if using), then leave to set for about 15 minutes. Use a clean palette knife to transfer each cake carefully to a paper case.

STORE These fancies will keep in the refrigerator for 1 day.

BAKER'S TIP
For a chocolate version, chill the filled squares well, then pierce each with a cocktail stick. Holding the stick, dip each cake into a bowl of melted dark chocolate (250g/9oz), then set on a wire rack. Once set, drizzle with melted white chocolate (50g/1¾oz) for a contrasting pattern.

Chocolate Fudge Cake Balls

The new must-have cakes to come out of the US. Deceptively simple to make, packet or leftover cake can also be used.

MAKES 20–25 | **35 MINS** | **25 MINS** | **4 WEEKS, UNDIPPED**

Chilling time
3 hrs, or 30 mins freezing

Special equipment
18cm (7in) round cake tin
food processor with blade attachment

Ingredients
100g (3½oz) unsalted butter, softened, or soft margarine, plus extra for greasing
100g (3½oz) caster sugar

2 eggs
80g (3oz) self-raising flour
20g (¾oz) cocoa powder
1 tsp baking powder
1 tbsp milk, plus extra if needed
150g (5½oz) ready-made chocolate fudge frosting (or use recipe for Chocolate Fudge Cake icing, see page 46)

250g (9oz) dark chocolate cake covering
50g (1¾oz) white chocolate

SMALL CAKES

1 Preheat the oven to 180°C (350°F/Gas 4). Grease the tin and line with baking parchment.

2 With an electric whisk, cream the butter and sugar until fluffy.

3 Beat in the eggs one at a time, mixing well between additions, until smooth and creamy.

4 Sift together the flour, cocoa, and baking powder, and fold into the cake batter.

5 Mix in enough milk to loosen the batter to a dropping consistency.

6 Spoon into the tin and bake for 25 minutes until the surface is springy to the touch.

7 Test with a skewer and then turn out onto a wire rack to cool completely.

8 Whiz the cake in a processor until it looks like breadcrumbs. Put 300g (10½oz) in a bowl.

9 Add the frosting and blend together to a smooth, uniform mix.

10 Using dry hands, roll the cake mix into balls, each the size of a walnut.

11 Put the balls on a plate and refrigerate for 3 hours or freeze for 30 minutes until firm.

12 Line 2 trays with parchment. Melt the cake covering according to directions on the packet.

13 Coat the balls in chocolate. Work quickly and if they start to break up, coat one at a time.

14 Using 2 forks, turn the balls in the chocolate until covered. Remove, allowing excess to drip.

15 Transfer the coated cake balls to the baking trays to dry. Continue to coat all the balls.

16 Melt the white chocolate in a bowl placed over a pan of boiling water.

17 Drizzle the white chocolate over the balls with a spoon, to decorate.

18 Leave the white chocolate to dry completely before transferring to a serving plate.
STORE The cake balls can be kept in an airtight container for 3 days.

Cake Ball variations

Strawberries and Cream Cake Pops

These are a fantastically impressive treat to serve at a children's party. You could even decorate a whole birthday cake with them.

MAKES 20–25 · **20 MINS** · **25 MINS** · **4 WEEKS, UNDIPPED**

Chilling time
3 hrs, or 30 mins freezing

Special equipment
18cm (7in) round cake tin
food processor with blade attachment
25 pieces of bamboo skewer, cut to
 approximately 10cm (4in) lengths,
 to resemble lollipop sticks

Ingredients
100g (3½oz) unsalted butter, softened,
 or soft margarine, plus extra for greasing
100g (3½oz) caster sugar
2 eggs
100g (3½oz) self-raising flour
1 tsp baking powder
150g (5½oz) ready-made buttercream frosting, or
 see vanilla buttercream, page 109, steps 13–15
2 tbsp good quality, smooth strawberry jam
250g (9oz) white chocolate cake covering

Method
1 Preheat the oven to 180°C (350°F/Gas 4). Grease the tin and line with parchment. Cream the butter or margarine, and sugar. Beat in the eggs one at a time, until the mixture is smooth. Sift the flour and baking powder together, and fold into the batter.

2 Pour the batter into the tin and bake for 25 minutes until the surface is springy to the touch. Turn out onto a wire rack to cool. Remove the parchment.

3 When the cake is cool, process it until it resembles breadcrumbs. Weigh out 300g (10½oz) of the crumbs and place in a bowl. Add the frosting and the jam, and mix thoroughly. Using dry hands, roll the mix into balls the size of a walnut. Put the balls on a plate and stick a skewer into each. Refrigerate for 3 hours or freeze for 30 minutes. Line 2 baking trays with parchment.

4 Melt the cake covering in a bowl set over simmering water. Dip the chilled balls one at a time into the molten chocolate, turning until completely covered, right up to the stick.

5 Gently take them out of the chocolate mixture and allow any excess to drip back into the bowl before transferring them to the baking trays to dry. The pops should be eaten on the same day.

BAKER'S TIP
To ensure a smooth, round finish to cake pops, cut an apple in half and place the halves cut side down on the lined baking tray. Dip the cake pops, then stick their bamboo skewers into the apple. This will help the cake pops dry without any marks to the surface.

Christmas Pudding Balls

I love to serve these cute little puddings at Christmas parties. An easy and delicious way to use up leftover Christmas pudding.

MAKES 15–20 · **20 MINS** · **25 MINS** · **4 WEEKS, UNDIPPED**

Chilling time
3 hrs, or 30 mins freezing

Special equipment
food processor with blade attachment

Ingredients
400g (14oz) leftover cooked Christmas Pudding,
 or Plum Pudding, see page 72
200g (5½oz) dark chocolate cake covering
50g (1¾oz) white chocolate cake covering
glacé cherries and candied angelica (optional)

Method
1 Whizz up the Christmas pudding in the processor until thoroughly broken up. Using dry hands roll the Christmas pudding mix into balls the size of a walnut. Put the balls on a plate and refrigerate them for 3 hours or freeze for 30 minutes until firm.

2 Line 2 baking trays with parchment paper. In a small, microwaveable bowl, heat the dark chocolate cake covering in bursts of 30 seconds for up to 2 minutes until melted, but not too hot. Alternatively, melt it in a small heatproof bowl over a saucepan of barely simmering water.

3 Take the balls out of the refrigerator a few at a time. Dip them into the molten chocolate, turning them with 2 forks until covered. Take them out of the chocolate mixture and transfer them to the lined baking sheets to dry.

4 Continue the process until all of the balls are coated. You will have to work quickly at this stage, as the chocolate can harden quite quickly, and the cake balls can disintegrate if left in the warm chocolate for too long.

5 Melt the white chocolate cake covering as above. Using a teaspoon drop a little of the white chocolate mixture on to the top of the Christmas pudding balls, so that it looks as if they have been drizzled with icing, or snow! The white chocolate should drip down the sides, but not cover the dark chocolate.

6 If you are feeling ambitious, slivers of glacé cherries and candied angelica can be cut to resemble holly leaves and berries, and stuck to the still molten white chocolate. Leave the balls until the white chocolate is hard.

STORE The pudding balls will keep in the refrigerator for 5 days.

White Chocolate and Coconut Snowballs

These coconut balls are sophisticated enough to serve as canapés.

MAKES 25–30 | 40 MINS | 25 MINS | 4 WEEKS, UNDIPPED

Chilling time
3 hrs, or 30 mins freezing

Special equipment
18cm (7in) round cake tin
food processor with blade attachment

Ingredients
100g (3½oz) unsalted butter, softened,
 or soft margarine, plus extra for greasing
100g (3½oz) caster sugar
2 eggs
100g (3½oz) self-raising flour
1 tsp baking powder
225g (8oz) ready-made buttercream frosting, or
 see vanilla buttercream, page 109, steps 13–15
225g (8oz) desiccated coconut
250g (9oz) white chocolate cake covering

Method

1 Preheat the oven to 180°C (350°F/Gas 4). Grease the tin and line the base with parchment. Cream the butter or margarine, and sugar until pale and fluffy. Beat in the eggs one at a time, beating well between each addition. Sift together the flour and baking powder, and fold into the cake batter.

2 Pour the batter into the tin and bake for 25 minutes. Turn out onto a wire rack to cool. Remove the baking parchment.

3 When the cake is cool, process until it resembles fine breadcrumbs. Weigh out 300g (10½oz) of the crumbs and put them in a bowl. Add the frosting and 75g (2½oz) of the desiccated coconut, and mix together.

4 Using dry hands, roll the mix into balls the size of a walnut. Refrigerate for 3 hours or freeze for 30 minutes. Line 2 baking trays with parchment and put the remaining coconut on a plate.

5 Melt the cake covering in a heatproof bowl over a pan of barely simmering water. Place the chilled cake balls, one at a time, into the melted chocolate mixture, using 2 forks to turn them until covered.

6 Transfer them to the plate of coconut. Roll them around in the coconut, then transfer to the baking tray to dry. You will have to work fast, as the chocolate can harden quickly, and the balls start to disintegrate if they are left in the chocolate too long.

STORE The cake balls will keep in a cool place in an airtight container for 2 days.

Whoopie Pies

Fast becoming a modern classic, whoopie pies are a quick and easy way to please a crowd.

| MAKES 10 PIES | 40 MINS | 12 MINS | 4 WEEKS, UNFILLED |

Ingredients
175g (6oz) unsalted butter, softened
150g (5½oz) soft light brown sugar
1 large egg
1 tsp vanilla extract
225g (8oz) self-raising flour
75g (2½oz) cocoa powder
1 tsp baking powder

150ml (5fl oz) whole milk
2 tbsp Greek yogurt or thick plain yogurt

For the vanilla buttercream
100g (3½oz) unsalted butter, softened
200g (7oz) icing sugar
2 tsp vanilla extract
2 tsp milk, plus extra if needed

To decorate
white and dark chocolate
200g (7oz) icing sugar

1 Preheat the oven to 180°C (350°F/Gas 4). Line several baking sheets with baking parchment.

2 With a whisk, cream together the butter and brown sugar until light and fluffy.

3 Add the egg and vanilla extract to the creamed mixture and beat in.

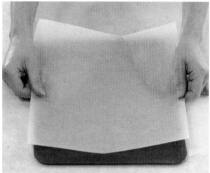

4 Beat the egg well to prevent curdling. The batter should appear smooth.

5 In a separate large bowl, sift together the flour, cocoa powder, and baking powder.

6 Gently fold a spoonful of the dry ingredients into the cake batter.

7 Add a little of the milk, mixing. Repeat until all the milk and dry ingredients are combined.

8 Blend in the thick yogurt, gently folding until well combined; this will moisten the pies.

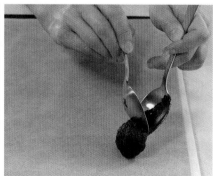

9 Place 20 heaped tablespoons of mixture on the lined baking sheets.

SMALL CAKES

10 Leave space for the mixture to spread out; each half will spread to 8cm (3in).

11 Dip a clean tablespoon in warm water and use it to smooth the surface of the halves.

12 Bake for around 12 minutes until a skewer comes out clean. Cool on a wire rack.

13 Using a wooden spoon, mix together the buttercream ingredients, except the mik.

14 Changing to a whisk, beat the mix for about 5 minutes until light and fluffy.

15 If the mixture seems stiff, loosen with extra milk to make the buttercream spreadable.

16 Spread a tablespoon of the buttercream onto each of the flat sides of half the cakes.

17 Sandwich together the iced with the un-iced halves to form the pies, pressing gently.

18 To decorate, use a vegetable peeler to produce white and dark chocolate shavings.

19 Place the icing sugar in a bowl and add 1–2 tablespoons water to form a thick paste.

20 Spoon the icing onto the top each pie, spreading it out for an even covering.

21 Lightly press the chocolate shavings onto the wet icing. **STORE** Will keep for 2 days.

Whoopie Pie variations

Peanut Butter Whoopie Pies

Sweet, salty, and creamy, these whoopie pies are addictive.

MAKES 10 PIES	40 MINS	12 MINS	4 WEEKS, UNFILLED

Ingredients

175g (6oz) unsalted butter, softened
150g (5½oz) soft light brown sugar
1 large egg
1 tsp vanilla extract
225g (8oz) self-raising flour
75g (2½oz) cocoa powder
1 tsp baking powder
150ml (5fl oz) whole milk, plus extra for the filling
2 tbsp Greek yogurt or thick plain yogurt
50g (1¾oz) cream cheese
50g (1¾oz) smooth peanut butter
200g (7oz) icing sugar, sifted

Method

1 Preheat the oven to 180°C (350°F/Gas 4). Line several large baking sheets with baking parchment. Place the butter and sugar in a bowl, and cream together until fluffy. Beat in the egg and vanilla extract.

2 In another bowl, sift in the flour, cocoa powder, and baking powder. Mix the dry ingredients and the milk into the batter a spoonful at a time. Fold in the yogurt.

3 Put heaped tablespoons of the batter onto the baking sheets, leaving space for the mixture to spread. Dip a tablespoon in warm water and use the back to smooth over the surface of the pies. Bake for 12 minutes, until well risen. Turn out on a wire rack to cool.

4 For the filling, beat the cream cheese and peanut butter until smooth. Cream in the sugar, adding a little milk if necessary to make a spreadable consistency. Spread onto each of the flat sides of half the cakes. Sandwich together with the un-iced cakes.

STORE The whoopie pies will keep in the refrigerator for 1 day.

Chocolate Orange Whoopie Pies

Rich, dark chocolate combined with the zesty tang of orange is a classic combination, used here to full advantage in these delicious little cakes.

MAKES 10 PIES	40 MINS	12 MINS	4 WEEKS, UNFILLED

Ingredients

275g (9½oz) unsalted butter, softened
150g (5½oz) soft light brown sugar
1 large egg
2 tsp vanilla extract
finely grated zest and juice of 1 orange
225g (8oz) self-raising flour
75g (2½oz) cocoa powder
1 tsp baking powder
150ml (5fl oz) whole milk or buttermilk
2 tbsp Greek yogurt or thick plain yogurt
200g (7oz) icing sugar

Method

1 Preheat the oven to 180°C (350°F/Gas 4). Line several baking sheets with parchment. Cream 175g (6oz) butter and brown sugar until fluffy. Beat in the egg and 1 teaspoon vanilla, and add the zest. In a bowl, sift the flour, cocoa, and baking powder. Mix the dry ingredients and the milk into the batter, in alternate spoonfuls. Fold in the yogurt.

2 Place heaped tablespoons onto the baking sheets, leaving space between them. Dip a spoon in warm water and use the back to smooth the surface of the cake mounds. Bake for 12 minutes until risen. Leave to cool slightly, then transfer to a wire rack.

3 For the buttercream, blend the remaining butter, icing sugar, 1 teaspoon vanilla extract, and orange juice, loosening with a little water. Spread 1 tablespoon of the filling onto the flat side of each cake half, and sandwich together with the remaining halves.

STORE The whoopie pies will keep in an airtight container for 2 days.

Coconut Whoopie Pies

This simple yet delicious variation uses the natural affinity between coconut and chocolate to great effect.

MAKES 10 PIES	40 MINS	12 MINS	4 WEEKS, UNFILLED

Ingredients

275g (9½oz) unsalted butter, softened
150g (5½oz) soft light brown sugar
1 large egg
2 tsp vanilla extract
225g (8oz) self-raising flour
75g (2½oz) cocoa powder
1 tsp baking powder
150ml (5fl oz) whole milk, plus extra for filling
2 tbsp Greek yogurt or thick plain yogurt
200g (7oz) icing sugar
5 tbsp desiccated coconut

Method

1 Preheat the oven to 180°C (350°F/Gas 4). Line several baking sheets with parchment. Cream 175g (6oz) butter and sugar until fluffy, and beat in the egg and 1 teaspoon vanilla extract. In a bowl, sift the flour, cocoa powder, and baking powder. Mix the dry ingredients and the milk into the batter alternately, a spoonful at a time. Fold in the yogurt.

2 Put tablespoons of batter onto the sheets. Dip a tablespoon in warm water and use the back to smooth over the surface of the pies. Bake for 12 minutes, until risen. Leave to cool slightly, then transfer to a wire rack. Soak the coconut in enough milk to cover it, for 10 minutes until softened. Drain in a sieve.

3 For the buttercream, whisk the remaining butter, icing sugar, vanilla, and 2 teaspoons milk until fluffy. Beat in the coconut. Spread the icing on half the cakes and sandwich with the remaining halves.

STORE The whoopie pies will keep in an airtight container for 2 days.

SMALL CAKES

Black Forest Whoopie Pies

A modern imitation of the famous gâteau, using tinned cherries.

| MAKES 10 PIES | 40 MINS | 12 MINS | 4 WEEKS, UNFILLED |

Ingredients

175g (6oz) unsalted butter, softened
150g (5½oz) soft light brown sugar
1 large egg
1 tsp vanilla extract
225g (8oz) self-raising flour
75g (2½oz) cocoa powder
1 tsp baking powder
150ml (5fl oz) whole milk or buttermilk
2 tbsp Greek yogurt or thick plain yogurt
225g (8oz) tinned black cherries, drained, or use frozen, defrosted
250g (9oz) mascarpone cheese
2 tbsp caster sugar

Method

1 Preheat the oven to 180°C (350°F/Gas 4). Line several baking sheets with parchment. Cream 175g (6oz) butter and brown sugar until fluffy. Beat in the egg and vanilla extract.

2 In a bowl, sift the flour, cocoa, and baking powder. Mix the dry ingredients and the milk into the batter, in alternate spoonfuls. Fold in the yogurt. Chop 100g (3½oz) of the cherries and fold these in too.

3 Place heaped tablespoons onto the baking sheets, leaving space between them. Dip a spoon in warm water and use the back to smooth the surface of the cakes. Bake for 12 minutes until well risen. Leave to cool slightly, then transfer to a wire rack.

4 Purée the remaining cherries until smooth. Mix the blended cherries and sugar into the mascarpone until well mixed; alternatively, leave a ripple effect in the filling. Spread 1 tablespoon of the filling onto the flat side of each cooled cake half, and sandwich together with the remaining halves.

STORE Best eaten the day of baking but can be stored for 1 day in the refrigerator.

Strawberries and Cream Whoopie Pies

Best served immediately, these strawberry layered whoopie pies make a lovely addition to a traditional afternoon tea.

| MAKES 10 PIES | 40 MINS | 12 MINS | 4 WEEKS, UNFILLED |

Ingredients

175g (6oz) unsalted butter, softened
150g (5½oz) soft light brown sugar
1 large egg
1 tsp vanilla extract
225g (8oz) self-raising flour
75g (2½oz) cocoa powder
1 tsp baking powder
150ml (8fl oz) whole milk
2 tbsp Greek yogurt or thick plain yogurt
150ml (5fl oz) double cream, whipped
250g (9oz) strawberries, thinly sliced
icing sugar, for dusting

Method

1 Preheat the oven to 180°C (350°F/Gas 4). Line several baking sheets with parchment. Cream the butter and sugar until fluffy. Beat in the egg and vanilla extract. In a bowl, sift together the flour, cocoa, and baking powder. Mix the dry ingredients and the milk into the batter alternately, a spoonful at a time. Fold in the yogurt.

2 Put heaped tablespoons of the batter onto the baking sheets, leaving space for the mixture to spread. Dip a tablespoon in warm water and use the back to smooth over the surface of the pies.

3 Bake for 12 minutes, until well risen. Leave the pies for a few minutes, then turn out onto a wire rack to cool.

4 Spread the cream onto half the cakes. Top with a layer of strawberries and a second cake. Dust with icing sugar and serve. These do not store and should be eaten on the day.

Chocolate Fondants

Usually thought of as a restaurant dessert, chocolate fondants are actually surprisingly easy to prepare at home.

SERVES 4	20 MINS	5–15 MINS	1 WEEK, UNBAKED

Special equipment
4 x 150ml (5fl oz) dariole moulds
or 10cm (4in) ramekins

Ingredients
150g (5½oz) unsalted butter, cubed,
  plus extra for greasing

1 heaped tbsp plain flour, plus extra for sprinkling
150g (5½oz) good-quality dark chocolate,
  broken into pieces
3 large eggs
75g (2½oz) caster sugar
cocoa powder or icing sugar, for dusting (optional)
cream or ice cream, to serve (optional)

Method

1 Preheat the oven to 200°C (400°F/Gas 6). Thoroughly grease the sides and base of each dariole mould or ramekin. Sprinkle the insides with a little flour, then turn the flour around in the dish until all the butter is covered with a thin layer of flour. Tip out the excess flour. Line the bases of the moulds with small discs of baking parchment.

2 Gently melt together the chocolate and butter in a heatproof bowl over simmering water, stirring occasionally. Make sure the base of the bowl does not touch the water. Cool slightly.

3 In a separate bowl, whisk together the eggs and sugar. Once the chocolate mixture has cooled slightly, beat it into the eggs and sugar until thoroughly combined. Sift the flour over the top of the mixture and gently fold it in.

4 Divide the mixture between the moulds, making sure that the mixture does not come right up to the top. At this stage the fondants can be refrigerated for several hours or overnight, as long as they are brought back to room temperature before cooking.

5 Cook the fondants in the middle of the oven for 5–6 minutes if using moulds, 12–15 minutes for ramekins. The sides should be firm, but the middles soft to the touch. Run a sharp knife around the edge of the moulds or ramekins. Turn the fondants out onto individual serving plates by putting a plate on top and inverting the whole thing. Gently remove each mould or ramekin and peel off the parchment.

6 Dust with cocoa powder or icing sugar, if desired, and serve immediately with cream or ice cream.

PREPARE AHEAD The uncooked mixture in the moulds or ramekins can be refrigerated overnight (see Baker's Tip).

BAKER'S TIP

Chocolate fondants are surprisingly simple to get right. They can be prepared up to a day in advance, which makes them a great dinner party dessert. Be sure to bring them back to room temperature before putting into the oven, or they may need cooking for slightly longer.

SMALL CAKES

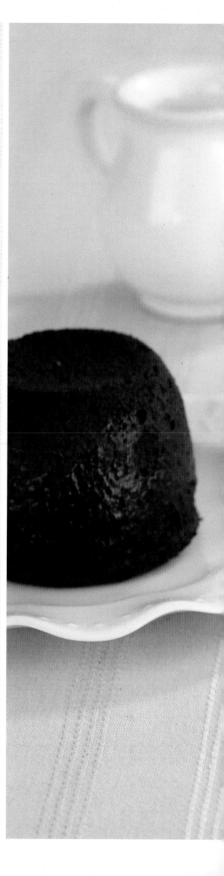

Lemon and Blueberry Muffins

These featherlight muffins are glazed with lemon juice for an extra burst of flavour. Best served warm.

MAKES 12   **20–25 MINS**   **15–20 MINS**   **UP TO 4 WEEKS**

Special equipment
12-hole muffin tin

Ingredients
60g (2oz) unsalted butter
280g (10oz) plain flour
1 tbsp baking powder
pinch of salt
200g (7oz) caster sugar
1 egg
finely grated zest and juice of 1 lemon

1 tsp vanilla extract
250ml (8fl oz) milk
225g (8oz) blueberries

1 Preheat the oven to 220°C (425°F/Gas 7). Melt the butter in a pan over a medium-low heat.

2 Sift the flour, baking powder, and salt into a bowl (do not make muffins in a food mixer).

3 Set 2 tablespoons sugar aside and stir the rest into the flour. Make a well in the centre.

4 In a separate bowl, beat the egg lightly until just broken down and mixed together.

5 Add the melted butter, lemon zest, vanilla, and milk. Beat the egg mixture until foamy.

6 In a slow, steady stream, pour the egg mixture into the well in the flour.

7 Stir with a rubber spatula, gradually drawing in the dry ingredients to make a smooth batter.

8 Gently fold in all the blueberries, taking care not to bruise any of the fruits.

9 Do not over-mix, or the muffins will be tough. Stop when the ingredients are blended.

10 Place the muffin cases in the tin. Spoon in the batter, filling to three-quarters full.

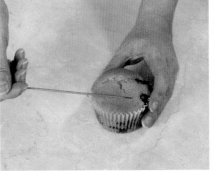

11 Bake for 15–20 minutes until a skewer inserted in the centre comes out clean.

12 Let the muffins cool slightly, then transfer them to a wire rack.

13 In a small bowl, stir the reserved sugar with the lemon juice until the sugar dissolves.

14 While the muffins are warm, dip the crown of each into the sugar and lemon mixture.

15 Set the muffins upright back on the wire rack and brush with any remaining glaze.

16 The warm muffins will absorb the maximum amount of the lemony glaze.
STORE Best served warm but will keep in an airtight container for 2 days.

Muffin variations

Chocolate Muffins

These muffins will fix chocolate cravings, and the buttermilk lends a delicious lightness.

MAKES 12	10 MINS	15 MINS	UP TO 8 WEEKS

Special equipment
12-hole muffin tin

Ingredients
225g (8oz) plain flour
60g (2oz) cocoa powder
1 tbsp baking powder
pinch of salt
115g (4oz) soft light brown sugar
150g (5½oz) chocolate chips
250ml (8fl oz) buttermilk
6 tbsp sunflower oil
½ tsp vanilla extract
2 eggs

Method
1 Preheat the oven to 200°C (400°F/Gas 6). Line the muffin tin with the paper cases and set aside. Sift the flour, cocoa powder, baking powder, and salt into a large bowl. Stir in the sugar and chocolate chips, and then make a well in the centre of the dry ingredients.

2 Beat together the buttermilk, oil, vanilla, and eggs, and pour the mixture into the centre of the dry ingredients. Mix together lightly to make a lumpy batter. Spoon the mixture into the paper cases, filling each three-quarters full.

3 Bake for 15 minutes or until well risen and firm to the touch. Immediately transfer the muffins to a wire rack and leave to cool.

STORE The muffins will keep in an airtight container for 2 days.

BAKER'S TIP
The use of liquid in these muffins, whether soured cream, buttermilk, or oil, will ensure a moist, longer-lasting cake. If a recipe calls for oil, make sure that you use a light, flavourless one such as sunflower or groundnut, to ensure that the delicious flavours of the muffins are not masked by the taste of the oil.

Lemon and Poppy Seed Muffins

Poppy seeds add a pleasing crunch to these delicate muffins.

MAKES 12	20–25 MINS	15–20 MINS	UP TO 4 WEEKS

Special equipment
12-hole muffin tin

Ingredients
60g (2oz) unsalted butter
280g (10oz) plain flour
1 tbsp baking powder
pinch of salt
200g (7oz) caster sugar, plus 2 tsp for sprinkling
1 egg, beaten
1 tsp vanilla extract
250ml (8fl oz) milk
2 tbsp poppy seeds
finely grated zest and juice of 1 lemon

Method
1 Preheat the oven to 220°C (425°F/Gas 7). Melt the butter in a pan over medium-low heat, then leave to cool slightly. Sift the flour, baking powder, and salt into a bowl. Stir in the sugar and make a well in the centre.

2 Put the egg in a separate bowl. Add in the melted butter, vanilla, and milk, and beat the mixture until foamy. Stir in the poppy seeds, and the lemon zest and juice.

3 Pour the egg mixture into the well in the flour. Stir to make a smooth batter, but do not over-mix. Stop as soon as the ingredients are blended.

4 Place muffin cases in the muffin tin. Spoon the batter evenly between the cases and sprinkle with 2 teaspoons of sugar.

5 Bake for 15–20 minutes until a skewer inserted in the centre of a muffin comes out clean. Let the muffins cool slightly, then transfer them (in their cases) to a wire rack to cool completely.

STORE The muffins will keep in an airtight container for 2 days.

Apple Muffins

These healthy muffins are best served straight from the oven.

| MAKES 12 | 10 MINS | 20–25 MINS | UP TO 8 WEEKS |

Special equipment
12-hole muffin tin

Ingredients
1 Golden Delicious apple, peeled, cored, and chopped
2 tsp lemon juice
115g (4oz) light demerara sugar, plus extra for sprinkling
200g (7oz) plain flour
85g (3oz) wholemeal flour
4 tsp baking powder
1 tbsp ground mixed spice
½ tsp salt
60g (2oz) pecan nuts, chopped
250ml (8fl oz) milk
4 tbsp sunflower oil
1 egg, beaten

Method
1 Preheat the oven to 200°C (400°F/Gas 6). Line the muffin tin with the paper cases and set aside. Put the apple in a bowl, add the lemon juice, and toss. Add 4 tablespoons of the sugar and set aside for 5 minutes.

2 Sift both the flours, baking powder, mixed spice, and salt into a large bowl, tipping in any bran left in the sieve. Stir in the sugar and pecans, then make a well in the centre of the dry ingredients.

3 Beat the milk, oil, and egg well, then add the apple. Tip the wet ingredients into the well of the flour and mix to a lumpy batter.

4 Spoon the mixture into the paper cases, filling each case three-quarters full. Bake the muffins for 20–25 minutes or until the tops are peaked and brown. Transfer all the muffins to a wire rack and sprinkle with extra sugar. Eat warm or cooled.

STORE The muffins will keep in an airtight container for 2 days.

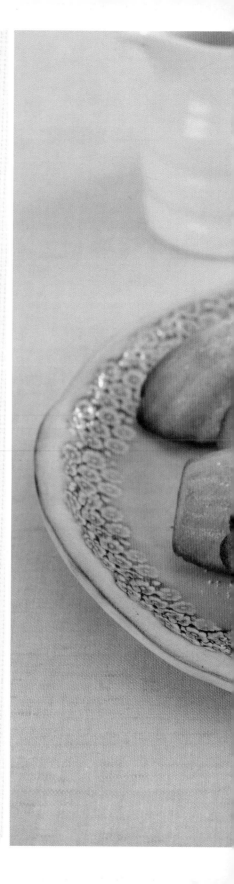

Madeleines

These elegant treats were made famous by French writer Marcel Proust, who took a bite and was transported back to his childhood.

| MAKES 12 | 15–20 MINS | 10 MINS | UP TO 4 WEEKS |

Special equipment
madeleine tin, or small 12-hole bun tin

Ingredients
60g (2oz) unsalted butter, melted and cooled, plus extra for greasing
60g (2oz) self-raising flour, sifted, plus extra for dusting
60g (2oz) caster sugar
2 eggs
1 tsp vanilla extract
icing sugar, for dusting

Method

1 Preheat the oven to 180°C (350°F/Gas 4). Carefully brush the tin with melted butter and dust with a little flour. Invert the tin and tap to remove excess flour.

2 Put the sugar, eggs, and vanilla into a mixing bowl. Using an electric whisk, mix for 5 minutes until the mixture is pale, thick, and holds a trail.

3 Sift the flour over the top and pour the melted butter down the side of the mixture. Using a large metal spoon, fold them in carefully and quickly, being careful not to knock out too much air.

4 Fill the moulds with the mixture and bake in the oven for 10 minutes. Remove from the oven and transfer to a wire rack to cool, before dusting with icing sugar.

STORE The madeleines will keep in an airtight container for 1 day.

BAKER'S TIP
These delightful little treats are meant to be as light as air. Care should be taken to incorporate as much air as possible into the batter at the whisking stage, and to lose as little volume from the batter when folding in the flour.

SMALL CAKES

Scones

Home-made scones are one of the simplest and best teatime treats. Buttermilk makes the lightest scones.

MAKES 6–8 | **15–20 MINS** | **12–15 MINS** | **UP TO 4 WEEKS**

Special equipment
7cm (2¾in) pastry cutter

Ingredients
60g (2oz) unsalted butter,
  chilled and cut into pieces,
  plus extra for greasing
250g (9oz) strong white bread flour,
  plus extra for dusting
2 tsp baking powder

½ tsp salt
175ml (6fl oz) buttermilk
butter, jam, and clotted or thick
  double cream, to serve (optional)

SMALL CAKES

1 Preheat the oven to 220°C (425°F/Gas 7). Line a baking sheet with parchment and grease.

2 Sift the flour, baking powder, and salt into a large chilled bowl.

3 Put the butter in the bowl, keeping all ingredients as cold as possible.

4 Rub with your fingertips until it forms fine crumbs, working quickly, lifting to aerate it.

5 Make a well in the centre and in a slow, steady stream, pour the buttermilk into it.

6 Quickly toss the flour mixture and buttermilk with a fork. Do not over-mix.

7 Stir the mixture till the crumbs form a dough. Add a little more buttermilk if it seems dry.

8 Turn onto a floured surface and knead for a few seconds. Keep it rough, not smooth.

9 Pat the dough out to a round 2cm (¾in) thick, keeping it as cool and unworked as you can.

10 Cut out rounds with the pastry cutter; see Baker's Tip, page 124.

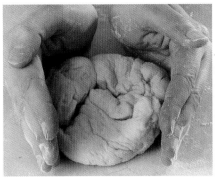

11 Pat out the trimmings and cut additional rounds until all the dough has been used.

12 Arrange the scones so they are about 5cm (2in) apart on the prepared baking sheet.

13 Bake in the preheated oven for 12–15 minutes until lightly browned and risen. Scones should be eaten the day they are baked, ideally still warm from the oven. Spread with butter, jam, and clotted cream or thick double cream.

Scone variations

Currant Scones

Serve these currant-studded scones straight from the oven, spread with butter or clotted cream.

| MAKES 6 | 15–20 MINS | 12–15 MINS | UP TO 4 WEEKS |

Ingredients

60g (2oz) unsalted butter, chilled and diced, plus extra for greasing
1 egg yolk, for glazing
175ml (6fl oz) buttermilk, plus 1 tbsp for glazing
250g (9oz) strong white bread flour, plus extra for dusting
2 tsp baking powder
½ tsp salt
¼ tsp bicarbonate of soda
2 tsp caster sugar
2 tbsp currants

Method

1 Preheat the oven to 220°C (425°F/Gas 7), and grease a baking sheet with butter. Beat the egg yolk and a tablespoon of buttermilk together, and set aside.

2 Sift the flour, baking powder, salt, and bicarbonate of soda into a bowl, and add the sugar. Add the butter and rub the mixture with your fingertips until it forms fine crumbs. Stir in the currants. Pour in the buttermilk and quickly toss the mixture with a fork to form crumbs. Stir just until the crumbs hold together and form a dough.

3 Transfer the dough to a floured work surface. Cut it in half and pat each half into a 15cm (6in) round, about 2cm (¾in) thick. With a sharp knife, cut each round into 4 wedges. Arrange the wedges about 5cm (2in) apart on the baking sheet, and brush with glaze.

4 Bake for 12–15 minutes, until lightly browned. Leave for a few minutes on the baking sheet, then transfer to a wire rack to cool. Best eaten warm the same day.

BAKER'S TIP

One of the secrets to well-risen scones is in the way they are cut. It is best to use a sharp pastry cutter, preferably made of metal, or sharp knife as here. They should be cut with a strong downward motion, and the cutter should not be twisted at all when cutting. This ensures a high, even rise on cooking.

Cheese and Parsley Scones

Basic scone mix is easily adapted for a tasty savoury variation.

| 20 SMALL OR 6 BIG | 20 MINS | 8–10 MINS | UP TO 12 WEEKS |

Special equipment

4cm (1½in) pastry cutter for small scones, or 6cm (2½in) pastry cutter for large scones

Ingredients

oil, for greasing
225g (8oz) plain flour, sifted, plus extra for dusting
1 tsp baking powder
pinch of salt
50g (1¾oz) unsalted butter, chilled and cubed
1 tsp dried parsley
1 tsp black peppercorns, crushed
50g (1¾oz) mature Cheddar cheese, grated
110ml (3½fl oz) milk

Method

1 Preheat the oven to 220°C (425°F/Gas 7). Lightly oil a medium-sized baking sheet. In a large bowl, mix together the flour, baking powder, and salt. Add the butter, and using your fingertips, rub it in until the mixture resembles fine breadcrumbs.

2 Stir in the parsley, pepper, and half the cheese. Then add enough milk to bind and make the dough come together (reserve the rest for brushing the tops of the scones). Lightly mix into a soft dough.

3 Roll out the dough on a lightly floured surface to a thickness of about 2cm (¾in). Using your chosen pastry cutter, cut out rounds (see Baker's Tip). Sit them on the prepared baking sheet, brush with the remaining milk, and sprinkle over the remaining cheese.

4 Bake on the top shelf of the oven for 8–10 minutes until golden. Leave on the baking sheet for a couple of minutes to cool a little, then either serve warm or cool completely on a wire rack. These scones are best eaten the same day.

Strawberry Shortcakes

These shortcakes are perfect served as a light summer dessert.

MAKES 6	15–20 MINS	12–15 MINS	4 WEEKS, UNFILLED

Special equipment
8cm (3in) pastry cutter

Ingredients
60g (2oz) unsalted butter, plus extra for greasing
250g (9oz) plain flour, sifted, plus extra for dusting
1 tbsp baking powder
½ tsp salt
45g (1½oz) caster sugar
175ml (6fl oz) double cream, plus extra if needed

For the coulis
500g (1lb 2oz) strawberries, hulled
2–3 tbsp icing sugar
2 tbsp Kirsch (optional)

For the filling
500g (1lb 2oz) strawberries, hulled and sliced
45g (1½oz) caster sugar, plus 2–3 tbsp
250ml (8fl oz) double cream
1 tsp vanilla essence

Method

1 Preheat the oven to 220°C (425°F/Gas 7). Butter a baking sheet. In a bowl, mix the flour, baking powder, salt, and sugar. Rub to form crumbs. Add cream, tossing; add more, if dry. Add the butter and rub in with your fingertips to form crumbs.

2 Press the crumbs together to form a ball of dough. On a floured surface, lightly knead the dough. Pat out a round, 1cm (½in) thick, and cut out 6 rounds with the cutter (see Baker's Tip). Transfer to the baking sheet and bake for 12–15 minutes. Cool on a wire rack.

3 For the coulis, purée the strawberries, then stir in the icing sugar and Kirsch (if using).

4 For the filling, mix the strawberries and sugar. Whip the cream until soft peaks form. Add 2–3 tablespoons of sugar and the vanilla. Whip until stiff. Cut the cakes in half. Put the strawberries on the bottom halves, followed by the cream. Top each with its lid. Pour the coulis around. Serve immediately.

Welsh Cakes

These traditional small cakes from Wales take minutes to prepare and cook, and you don't even have to remember to preheat the oven.

| 24 SMALL CAKES | 20 MINS | 16–24 MINS | UP TO 4 WEEKS |

Special equipment
5cm (2in) pastry cutter

Ingredients
200g (7oz) self-raising flour,
 plus extra for dusting
100g (3½oz) unsalted butter,
 chilled and diced, plus extra for frying
75g (2½oz) caster sugar, plus extra for dusting
75g (2½oz) sultanas
1 large egg, beaten
a little milk, if needed

Method

1 Sift the flour into a large bowl. Rub the butter into the flour until the mixture resembles fine breadcrumbs. Mix in the sugar and the sultanas. Pour in the egg.

2 Mix the ingredients together, bringing the mixture into a ball using your hands. This should be firm enough to roll out, but if it seems too stiff add a little milk.

3 On a floured work surface, roll out the dough to about 5mm (¼in) thick and cut out disks, using the pastry cutter.

4 Heat a large, heavy frying pan, cast iron skillet, or flat griddle over medium-low heat. Fry the cakes, in batches, in a little melted butter for 2–3 minutes on each side, until they puff up, are golden brown, and cooked through.

5 While still warm, generously dust the cakes with a little caster sugar, before serving. Welsh cakes are best eaten immediately. If you freeze them, reheat in the oven after defrosting.

BAKER'S TIP
Welsh cakes are an easy afternoon treat, and can be ready to eat within minutes. Cook them over fairly low heat, and be extremely careful when turning them over to cook on the second side as the self-raising flour makes them very fragile at this stage. Delicious eaten immediately with butter.

SMALL CAKES

Rock Cakes

It's high time these classic British buns enjoyed a renaissance. Correctly cooked, they are light, crumbly, and incredibly simple to make.

MAKES 12	15 MINS	15–20 MINS	UP TO 4 WEEKS

Ingredients

200g (7oz) self-raising flour
pinch of salt
100g (3½oz) unsalted butter, chilled and diced
75g (2½oz) caster sugar
100g (3½oz) mixed dried fruit
  (raisins, sultanas, and mixed peel)
2 eggs
2 tbsp milk, plus extra if needed
½ tsp vanilla extract
butter or jam, to serve (optional)

Method

1 Preheat the oven to 190°C (375°F/Gas 5). In a large bowl, rub together the flour, salt, and butter until the mixture resembles fine breadcrumbs. Mix in the sugar. Add the dried fruit and mix throughly.

2 In a jug, whisk together the eggs, milk, and vanilla extract. Make a well in the centre of the flour mixture and pour the egg mixture into it. Combine thoroughly to produce a firm mixture. Use a little more milk if the mixture seems too stiff.

3 Line 2 baking sheets with parchment. Place large heaped tablespoons of the mixture onto the baking sheets, leaving space for the cakes to spread. Bake in the centre of the oven for 15–20 minutes until golden brown.

4 Remove to a wire rack to cool slightly. Split and serve warm, split. Spread with butter or jam. Rock cakes should be eaten the day they are baked as they do not store well.

BAKER'S TIP

These easy-to-make cakes are named after their classic, rugged shape, rather than their texture! Make sure that the mixture is piled at least 5–7cm (2–3in) high on the baking sheet, which will ensure the classic rough edges even after they have spread out on baking.

Profiteroles

These cream-filled choux pastry buns, drizzled with chocolate sauce, make a deliciously decadent dessert.

SERVES 4 | **30 MINS** | **22 MINS** | **12 WEEKS, UNFILLED**

Ingredients
60g (2oz) plain flour
50g (1¾oz) unsalted butter
2 eggs, beaten

For the filling and topping
400ml (14fl oz) double cream
200g (7oz) good-quality dark
  chocolate, broken into pieces
25g (scant 1oz) butter
2 tbsp golden syrup

Special equipment
2 piping bags with a 1cm (½in) plain
nozzle and 5mm (¼in) star nozzle

SMALL CAKES

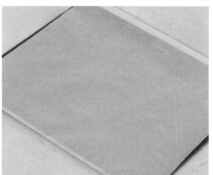

1 Preheat the oven to 220°C (425°F/Gas 7). Line 2 large baking trays with parchment.

2 Sift the flour into a large bowl, holding the sieve up high to aerate the flour.

3 Put the butter and 150ml (5fl oz) water into a small saucepan and heat gently until melted.

4 Bring to a boil, remove from the heat, and tip in the flour all at once.

5 Beat with a wooden spoon until smooth; the mixture should form a ball. Cool for 10 minutes.

6 Gradually add the eggs, beating very well after each addition to incorporate.

7 Continue adding the egg, little by little, to form a stiff, smooth, and shiny paste.

8 Spoon the mixture into a piping bag fitted with a 1cm (½in) plain nozzle.

9 Pipe walnut-sized rounds, set well apart. Bake for 20 minutes until risen and golden.

10 Remove from the oven and slit the side of each bun to allow the steam to escape.

11 Return to the oven for 2 minutes, to crisp, then transfer to a wire rack to cool completely.

12 Before serving, pour 100ml (3½fl oz) cream into a pan and whip the rest until just peaking.

13 Add the chocolate, butter, and syrup to the cream in the pan and heat gently until melted.

14 Pile the whipped cream into a piping bag fitted with a 5mm (¼in) star nozzle.

15 Pipe cream into each bun. Open the buns and fill them with the cream.

16 Arrange the buns on a serving plate or cake stand. Stir the sauce, pour it over, and serve immediately. **PREPARE AHEAD** The unfilled buns will keep in an airtight container for 2 days.

Choux Pastry variations

Chocolate Orange Profiteroles

A delicious twist on the original, heightened by sharp orange zest and liqueur. Try to use dark chocolate that is at least 60 per cent cocoa solids for a bitter chocolate orange taste.

| SERVES 6 | 20 MINS | 40 MINS | 12 WEEKS, UNFILLED |

Special equipment
2 piping bags with a 1cm (½in) plain nozzle and 5mm (¼in) star nozzle

Ingredients

For the choux buns
60g (2oz) plain flour
50g (1¾oz) unsalted butter
2 eggs, beaten

For the filling
500ml (16fl oz) double cream or whipping cream
finely grated zest of 1 large orange
2 tbsp Grand Marnier

For the chocolate sauce
150g (5½oz) good-quality dark chocolate, broken into pieces
300ml (10fl oz) single cream
2 tbsp golden syrup
1 tbsp Grand Marnier

Method

1 Preheat the oven to 220°C (425°F/Gas 7). Line 2 large baking trays with parchment. Sift the flour into a large bowl, holding the sieve up high to aerate the flour.

2 Put the butter and 150ml (5fl oz) water into a small pan and heat gently until melted. Bring to a boil, remove from the heat, and tip in the flour. Beat with a wooden spoon until smooth; the mixture should form a ball. Cool for 10 minutes. Gradually add the eggs, beating well after each addition to incorporate. Continue adding the egg, little by little, to form a stiff and smooth paste.

3 Spoon the mixture into a piping bag fitted with a 1cm (½in) plain nozzle. Pipe walnut-sized rounds, set well apart. Bake for 20 minutes until risen and golden. Remove from the oven and slit the side of each bun to allow the steam to escape. Return to the oven for 2 minutes, to crisp, then transfer to a wire rack to cool completely.

4 To make the filling, whisk the cream, orange zest, and Grand Marnier in a bowl until just thicker than soft peaks. Fill the profiteroles with the cream using the piping bag with star nozzle.

5 To make the chocolate sauce, melt the chocolate, cream, syrup, and Grand Marnier together in a small pan, whisking until the sauce is smooth and glossy. Serve the profiteroles with the hot sauce spooned over.

PREPARE AHEAD The unfilled buns will keep in an airtight container for 2 days.

BAKER'S TIP
Immediately after removing choux pastries from the oven, it is vital to create a slit in each to allow the steam to escape. This will result in an open-textured, dry, and crisp pastry. If you do not slit the pastries, the steam will remain inside and the buns will be soggy.

Cheese Gougères with Smoked Salmon

These savoury choux pastry puffs are a traditional dish of the Burgundy region of France, where they are displayed in almost every bakery window. Stuffed with smoked salmon they make sophisticated canapés.

| SERVES 8 | 40–45 MINS | 30–35 MINS |

Ingredients
75g (2½oz) unsalted butter, plus extra for greasing
1¼ tsp salt
150g (5½oz) plain flour, sifted
6 eggs
125g (4½oz) Gruyère cheese, coarsely grated

For the smoked salmon filling
salt and pepper
1kg (2¼lb) fresh spinach, trimmed and washed
30g (1oz) unsalted butter
1 onion, finely chopped
4 garlic cloves, finely chopped
pinch of ground nutmeg
250g (9oz) cream cheese
175g (6oz) smoked salmon, sliced into strips
4 tbsp milk

Method

1 Preheat the oven to 190°C (375°F/Gas 5). Grease 2 baking sheets. Melt the butter in a pan with 250ml (8fl oz) water and ¾ teaspoon of salt. Bring to a boil. Remove from the heat and add the flour. Beat until smooth. Return the pan to the stove and beat over low heat for 30 seconds, to dry.

2 Remove from the heat. Add 4 eggs, 1 at a time, beating well. Beat the fifth egg; add gradually. Stir in half the cheese. Place eight 6cm (2½in) mounds of dough on the baking sheets. Beat the remaining egg and salt. Brush over each of the puffs. Sprinkle with the remaining cheese. Bake for 30–35 minutes until firm. Remove and transfer to a wire rack. Slice the tops and leave to cool.

3 Bring a pan of salted water to a boil. Add the spinach, and wilt for 1–2 minutes. Drain. When cool, squeeze to remove water, then chop. Melt the butter in a frying pan. Add the onion and cook until soft. Add the garlic, nutmeg, salt and pepper to taste, and the spinach. Cooking, stirring, until any liquid has evaporated. Add the cream cheese and stir until the mixture is thoroughly combined. Remove from the heat.

4 Add two-thirds of the smoked salmon, pour in the milk, and stir. Mound 2–3 tablespoons of filling into each cheese puff. Arrange the remaining smoked salmon on top. Rest the lid against the side of each filled puff and serve at once.

SMALL CAKES

Chocolate Éclairs

These cousins of the profiterole can be easily adapted: try the chocolate orange topping and orange cream filling (see opposite), or filling with crème pâtissière or chocolate crème pâtissière.

| MAKES 30 | 30 MINS | 25–30 MINS | 12 WEEKS, UNFILLED |

Special equipment
piping bag with 1cm (½in) plain nozzle

Ingredients
75g (2½oz) unsalted butter
125g (4½oz) plain flour, sifted
3 eggs
500ml (16fl oz) double cream
 or whipping cream
150g (5½oz) good-quality dark chocolate,
 broken into pieces

Method
1 Preheat the oven to 200°C (400°F/Gas 6). Melt the butter in a pan with 200ml (7fl oz) cold water, then bring to the boil, remove from the heat, and stir in the flour. Beat with a wooden spoon until well combined.

2 Lightly beat the eggs and add to the flour and butter mixture a little at a time, whisking constantly. Continue whisking until the mixture is smooth and glossy and comes away easily from the sides of the pan. Transfer to the piping bag.

3 Pipe 10cm (4in) lengths of the mixture onto 2 baking trays lined with baking parchment, cutting the end of the length of pastry from the bag with a wet knife. You should have around 30 in all. Bake for 20–25 minutes or until golden brown, then remove from the oven and make a slit down the side of each.

Return to the oven for 5 minutes for the insides to cook through. Then remove and leave to cool.

4 Put the cream in a mixing bowl and beat with an electric hand whisk until soft peaks form. Spoon or pipe into each éclair. Place the chocolate pieces in a heatproof bowl. Sit the bowl over a pan of simmering water, making sure the bowl does not touch the water, and leave the chocolate to melt. Spoon over the éclairs and leave to dry before serving.

PREPARE AHEAD The unfilled éclairs will keep in an airtight container for 2 days.

Raspberry Cream Meringues

These mini meringues are filled with fresh raspberries and whipped cream, perfect for a summer buffet.

MAKES 6–8 | 10 MINS | 1 HOUR

Special equipment
metal mixing bowl
piping bag with plain nozzle
(optional)

Ingredients
4 egg whites, at room temperature
(each medium egg white will
weigh about 30g/1oz)
about 240g (8¾oz) caster sugar,
see step 3

For the filling
100g (3½oz) raspberries
300ml (10fl oz) double cream
1 tbsp icing sugar, sifted

1 Preheat the oven to around 120°C (250°F/Gas ¼). Line a baking sheet with parchment.

2 Ensure the bowl is clean and dry; use a lemon to remove traces of grease, if need be.

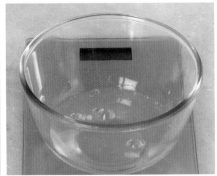

3 Weigh the egg whites. You will need exactly double the weight of sugar to egg whites.

4 Whisk the egg whites in the metal bowl until they are stiff and form strong peaks.

5 Gradually add half the sugar, a couple of tablespoons at a time, whisking in between.

6 Gently fold the remaining sugar into the egg whites, trying to lose as little air as possible.

7 Put tablespoons of the mixture onto the baking tray leaving 5cm (2in) gaps between.

8 Alternatively, pipe with a plain nozzle. Bake in the centre of the oven for 1 hour.

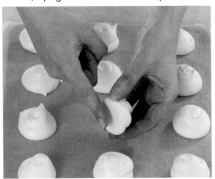

9 They are ready when they lift easily from the parchment and sound hollow when tapped.

10 Turn off the oven and leave the meringues to cool inside. Remove to a wire rack until cold.

11 Put the raspberries in a bowl and crush them with the back of a fork, so they break up.

12 In a separate bowl whisk up the double cream until firm but not stiff.

13 Gently fold together the cream and crushed raspberries, and combine with the icing sugar.

14 Spread a little of the raspberry mixture onto half the meringues.

15 Top with the remaining meringue halves and gently press together to form sandwiches.

For sweet canapés, pipe smaller meringues and reduce the cooking time to 45 minutes; makes about 20 sandwiches. **PREPARE AHEAD** Keep unfilled in an airtight container for 5 days.

Meringue variations

Giant Pistachio Meringues

Too large to sandwich with cream, these beautiful creations are eaten like oversized biscuits.

MAKES 8   15 MINS   1½ HOURS

Special equipment
food processor with blade attachment
large metal mixing bowl

Ingredients
100g (3½oz) unsalted, shelled pistachio nuts
4 egg whites, at room temperature
about 240g (8¾oz) caster sugar,
  see page 134, step 3

Method
1 Preheat the oven to the lowest setting, around 120°C (250°F/Gas ¼). Spread the pistachio nuts on a baking sheet and bake for 5 minutes, then turn them out into a tea towel and rub to remove excess skin. Cool. Finely grind just less than half the nuts in a food processor, and roughly chop the rest.

2 Put the egg whites into the metal bowl and whisk with an electric whisk until stiff peaks form. Add the sugar 2 tablespoons at a time, whisking between each addition, until you have added at least half. Fold in the remaining sugar, and the ground pistachios, trying to lose as little air as possible.

3 Line a baking sheet with parchment. Put large heaped tablespoons of the meringue mixture on to the sheet, leaving at least 5cm (2in) gaps between them. Scatter the tops with the chopped pistachios.

4 Bake in the centre of the oven for 1½ hours. Turn off the oven and leave the meringues to cool inside, to help stop them cracking. Remove the meringues from the oven to a wire rack to cool completely. Serve the meringues piled on top of each other, for maximum impact.

STORE The meringues will keep in an airtight container for 3 days.

Lemon and Praline Meringues

Similar to Monts Blancs (see right), these have added crunch.

SERVES 6   35 MINS   1½ HOURS

Special equipment
piping bag with star nozzle

Ingredients
3 egg whites, at room temperature
about 180g (6oz) caster sugar,
  see page 134, step 3
vegetable oil, for greasing
60g (2oz) granulated sugar
60g (2oz) whole blanched almonds
pinch of cream of tartar
85g (3oz) dark chocolate, broken up
150ml (5fl oz) double cream
3 tbsp lemon curd

Method
1 Preheat the oven to 120°C (250°F/Gas ¼) and line a baking sheet with parchment. Whisk the egg whites until stiff. Add 2 tablespoons caster sugar, and whisk until smooth and shiny. Add sugar, 1 tablespoon at a time, whisking well after each addition. Spoon into the piping bag, and pipe six 10cm (4in) circles onto the baking sheet. Bake for 1½ hours or until crisp.

2 Meanwhile, make the praline. Oil a baking sheet and put the granulated sugar, almonds, and cream of tartar into a small, heavy saucepan. Set the pan over a gentle heat and stir until the sugar dissolves. Boil until the syrup turns golden, then pour out onto the greased baking sheet. Leave until completely cold, then coarsely chop.

3 Melt the chocolate in a bowl set over simmering water. Whip the cream until just holding a trail, and fold in the lemon curd. Spread each meringue with chocolate. Allow to set, then pile the lemon curd cream on top, sprinkle with praline, and serve.

PREPARE AHEAD The meringue bases will keep in an airtight container for 5 days.

Monts Blancs

If using sweetened chestnut purée, omit the caster sugar in the filling.

MAKES 8   **20 MINS**   **45–60 MINS**

Special equipment
large metal mixing bowl
10cm (4in) pastry cutter

Ingredients
4 egg whites, at room temperature
about 240g (8¾oz) caster sugar,
   see page 134, step 3
sunflower oil, for greasing

For the filling
435g can sweetened or unsweetened
   chestnut purée
100g (3½oz) caster sugar (optional)
1 tsp vanilla extract
500ml (16fl oz) double cream
icing sugar, for dusting

Method
1 Preheat the oven to the lowest setting, around 120°C (250°F/Gas ¼). Put the egg whites into a large, clean metal bowl and whisk them until they are stiff, and leave peaks when the whisk is removed from the egg whites. Gradually add the sugar 2 tablespoons at a time, whisking well between each addition, until you have added at least half. Gently fold the remaining sugar into the egg whites, trying to lose as little air as possible.

2 Lightly grease the pastry cutter. Line 2 baking sheets with silicone paper. Place the pastry cutter on the sheets, and spoon the meringue mixture into the ring, to a depth of 3cm (1¼in). Smooth over the top and gently remove the ring. Repeat until there are 4 meringue bases on each baking sheet.

3 Bake the meringues in the centre of the oven for 45 minutes if you like them chewy, otherwise bake for 1 hour. Turn off the oven and leave the meringues to cool inside, to stop them cracking. Remove to a wire rack to cool completely.

4 Put the chestnut purée in a bowl with the caster sugar (if using), vanilla extract, and

4 tablespoons of double cream, and beat together until smooth. Push through a fine sieve to make a light, fluffy filling. In a separate bowl, whisk up the remaining double cream until firm.

5 Gently smooth 1 tablespoon chestnut filling over the top of the meringues, using a palette knife to smooth the surface level. Top each meringue with a spoonful of whipped cream, smoothed round with a palette knife to give the appearance of soft peaks. Dust with icing sugar and serve.

PREPARE AHEAD The meringue bases can be prepared 5 days ahead and stored in an airtight container.

BAKER'S TIP
Make sure that the bowl you are using to whisk the egg whites in is completely clean and dry. For absolute accuracy, it is best to weigh the egg whites. You will need precisely double the weight of sugar to egg whites. An electronic scale is best.

biscuits cookies & slices

Hazelnut and Raisin Oat Cookies

These biscuits are an ideal cookie jar staple – tasty enough to please the kids and healthy enough for the adults.

MAKES 18 · **20 MINS** · **10–15 MINS** · **UP TO 8 WEEKS**

Ingredients

100g (3½oz) hazelnuts
100g (3½oz) unsalted butter, softened
200g (7oz) soft light brown sugar
1 egg, beaten
1 tsp vanilla extract
1 tbsp runny honey

125g (4½oz) self-raising flour, sifted
125g (4½oz) jumbo porridge oats
pinch of salt
100g (3½oz) raisins
a little milk, if needed

1 Preheat the oven to 190°C (375°F/Gas 5). Toast the nuts on a baking sheet for 5 minutes.

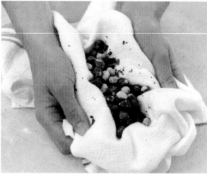

2 Once toasted, rub with a clean tea towel to remove most of the skins.

3 Roughly chop the hazelnuts and then set aside.

4 In a bowl, cream together the butter and sugar with an electric whisk until smooth.

5 Add the egg, vanilla extract, and honey, and beat well until smooth once more.

6 Combine the flour, oats, and salt in a separate bowl, and stir to mix.

7 Stir the flour mixture into the creamed mixture and beat until very well combined.

8 Add the chopped nuts and raisins, and mix until evenly distributed throughout.

9 If the mixture is too stiff to work with easily, add a little milk until it becomes pliable.

10 Line 2 or 3 baking sheets with parchment. Roll the dough into walnut-sized balls.

11 Flatten each ball slightly, leaving plenty of space between them.

12 Bake in batches for 10–15 minutes until golden. Cool slightly, then move to a wire rack.

13 Leave to cool completely before serving. **STORE** The cookies will keep in an airtight container for 5 days, so if you make a batch on Sunday night they will last the school and working week.

Cookie variations

Pistachio and Cranberry Oat Cookies

The jewel colours of the pistachios and cranberries gleam out from these slightly more grown up versions of the classic fruit and nut cookies.

MAKES 24   **20 MINS**   **10–15 MINS**   **UP TO 8 WEEKS**

Ingredients
100g (3½oz) unsalted butter, softened
200g (7oz) soft light brown sugar
1 egg
1 tsp vanilla extract
1 tbsp runny honey
125g (4½oz) self-raising flour, sifted
125g (4½oz) oats
pinch of salt
100g (3½oz) pistachio nuts, lightly toasted and roughly chopped.
100g (3½oz) dried cranberries, roughly chopped
a little milk, if needed

Method
1 Preheat the oven to 190°C (375°F/Gas 5). Put the butter and sugar in a bowl, and cream with an electric whisk until smooth. Add the egg, vanilla extract, and honey, and beat well until smooth.

2 Add the flour, oats, and salt, stirring with a wooden spoon to combine. Add the chopped nuts and cranberries and mix until thoroughly combined. If the mixture is too stiff, add a little milk until it becomes pliable.

3 Take walnut-sized pieces and roll them into a ball between your palms. Place on 2 or 3 baking sheets lined with parchment and flatten them slightly, leaving space for the biscuits to spread.

4 Bake for 10–15 minutes until golden brown (you may need to do this in batches). Leave on the tray to cool slightly before transferring to a wire rack.

STORE The cookies will keep in an airtight container for 5 days.

BAKER'S TIP
Once you have mastered the recipe for oatmeal cookies, try experimenting with different combinations of fresh or dried fruit and nuts, or adding seeds such as sunflower seeds and pumpkin seeds into the mix.

Apple and Cinnamon Oat Cookies

Adding grated apple to the dough makes these cookies soft and chewy.

MAKES 24   **20 MINS**   **10–15 MINS**   **UP TO 8 WEEKS**

Ingredients
100g (3½oz) unsalted butter, softened
200g (7oz) soft light brown sugar
1 egg
1 tsp vanilla extract
1 tbsp runny honey
125g (4½oz) self-raising flour, sifted
125g (4½oz) oats
2 tsp cinnamon
pinch of salt
2 apples, peeled, cored, and finely grated
a little milk, if needed

Method
1 Preheat the oven to 190°C (375°F/Gas 5). Put the butter and sugar in a bowl and cream together with an electric whisk until smooth. Add the egg, vanilla extract, and honey, and beat well until smooth.

2 With a wooden spoon, stir the flour, oats, cinnamon, and salt into the creamed mixture to combine. Mix in the apple. If the mixture seems too stiff, add a little milk. Take walnut-sized pieces of dough and roll them into a ball between your palms.

3 Place on 2 or 3 baking sheets lined with parchment and flatten slightly, leaving space for the biscuits to spread.

4 Bake for 10–15 minutes until golden brown. Leave to cool slightly and then transfer to a wire rack to cool completely.

STORE The cookies will keep in an airtight container for 5 days.

White Chocolate and Macadamia Nut Cookies

Here classic chocolate cookies are given a sophisticated twist.

| MAKES 24 | 25 MINS | 10–15 MINS | UP TO 4 WEEKS |

Chilling time
30 mins

Ingredients

150g (5½oz) good-quality dark chocolate, broken into pieces
100g (3½oz) self-raising flour
25g (scant 1oz) cocoa powder
75g (2½oz) unsalted butter, softened
175g (6oz) soft light brown sugar
1 egg, beaten
1 tsp vanilla extract
50g (1¾oz) macadamia nuts, roughly chopped
50g (1¾oz) white chocolate chunks

Method

1 Preheat the oven to 180°C (350°F/Gas 4). Melt the chocolate in a heatproof bowl set over a pan of simmering water. The bowl should not touch the water. Set aside to cool. Sift the flour and cocoa together.

2 In a large bowl, cream together the butter and sugar with an electric whisk until light and fluffy. Beat in the egg and vanilla extract. Fold in the flour mixture. Add the chocolate and mix thoroughly to combine. Finally, fold in the macadamia nuts and white chocolate chunks. Cover the bowl and chill for 30 minutes.

3 Place tablespoons of the chilled cookie dough on 2 or 3 baking sheets lined with parchment, positioned at least 5cm (2in) apart, as they will spread.

4 Bake in the top third of the oven for 10–15 minutes until cooked through but still soft in the middle. Leave on the trays for a few minutes, then transfer to a wire rack to cool.

STORE The cookies will keep in an airtight container for 3 days.

Butter Biscuits

These thin, elegant biscuits are one of my favourite recipes. They are quick, simple, and decidedly moreish.

MAKES 30 | **15 MINS** | **10–15 MINS** | **UP TO 8 WEEKS**

Special equipment
7cm (2¾in) round pastry cutter
food processor with blade attachment (optional)

Ingredients
100g (3½oz) caster sugar
225g (8oz) plain flour, sifted, plus extra for dusting
150g (5½oz) unsalted butter, softened and diced
1 egg yolk
1 tsp vanilla extract

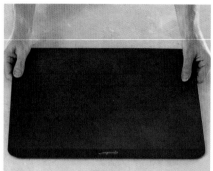

1 Preheat the oven to 180°C (350°F/Gas 4). Have several non-stick baking sheets to hand.

2 Put the sugar, flour, and butter into a large bowl, or into the bowl of a food processor.

3 Rub together, or pulse-blend, the ingredients until they look like fine breadcrumbs.

4 Add the egg yolk and vanilla extract, and bring the mixture together into a dough.

5 Turn the dough out onto a lightly floured work surface and knead it briefly until smooth.

6 Flour the dough and work surface well, and roll it out to a thickness of about 5mm (¼in).

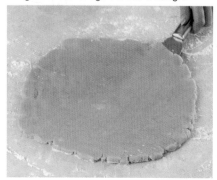

7 Use a palette knife to move the dough around, to prevent sticking.

8 If the dough is too sticky to roll well, chill for 15 minutes, then try again.

9 With the pastry cutter, cut out round biscuits and transfer them to the baking sheets.

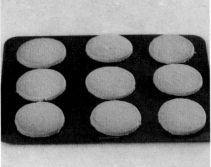

10 Re-roll the pastry offcuts to 5mm (¼in) thick. Cut out biscuits until all the dough is used.

11 Bake in batches for 10–15 minutes until golden brown at the edges.

12 Leave the biscuits to cool until firm enough to handle, then transfer to a wire rack.

13 Leave the butter biscuits to cool completely on the wire rack, before serving. **STORE** The biscuits will keep well in an airtight container for 5 days.

Butter Biscuit variations

Crystallized Ginger Biscuits

Here crystallized ginger adds warmth and depth of flavour.

MAKES 30 | 15 MINS | 12–15 MINS | UP TO 8 WEEKS

Special equipment
7cm (3in) round pastry cutter
food processor with blade attachment (optional)

Ingredients
100g (3½oz) caster sugar
225g (8oz) plain flour, sifted, plus extra for dusting
150g (5½oz) unsalted butter, softened and diced
1 tsp ground ginger
50g (1¾oz) crystallized ginger, finely chopped
1 egg yolk
1 tsp vanilla extract

Method
1 Preheat the oven to 180°C (350°F/Gas 4). Have 3 or 4 non-stick baking sheets to hand. Combine the sugar, flour, and butter in a bowl, or in the bowl of a food processor fitted with a blade, and rub or process together until the mixture forms crumbs. Stir in the ground and crystallized gingers.

2 Add the egg yolk and vanilla extract, and bring the mixture together into a dough. Turn out onto a lightly floured work surface and knead it briefly until smooth.

3 Flour the dough and work surface well, and roll it out to 5mm (¼in) thick. Cut out biscuit shapes with the pastry cutter and transfer them to the baking sheets.

4 Bake in the oven for 12–15 minutes until golden brown at the edges. Leave on the baking sheets for a few minutes, then transfer to a wire rack to cool completely.

STORE The biscuits will keep in an airtight container for 5 days.

Almond Butter Biscuits

The addition of almond extract makes these delicious biscuits quite grown up and not overly sweet.

MAKES 30 | 15 MINS | 12–15 MINS | UP TO 8 WEEKS

Special equipment
7cm (3in) round pastry cutter
food processor with blade attachment (optional)

Ingredients
100g (3½oz) caster sugar
225g (8oz) plain flour, sifted, plus extra for dusting
150g (5½oz) unsalted butter, softened and diced
40g (1½oz) flaked almonds, lightly toasted
1 egg yolk
1 tsp almond extract

Method
1 Preheat the oven to 180°C (350°F/Gas 4). Have 3 or 4 non-stick baking sheets to hand. Mix the sugar, flour, and butter in a bowl, or in the bowl of a food processor with a blade attachment. Rub or process together until it forms crumbs. Mix in the almonds.

2 Add the egg yolk and almond essence, and bring the mixture together into a dough. Knead briefly until smooth and roll out to 5mm (¼in) thick.

3 Cut out biscuit shapes with the cutter and transfer to the baking sheets. Bake in batches for 12–15 minutes until golden brown at the edges. Leave for a few minutes, then transfer to a wire rack to cool.

STORE The biscuits will keep in an airtight container for 5 days.

BAKER'S TIP
Always look for almond extract, as bottles labelled "essence" are made from synthetic flavourings. For excellent after-dinner biscuits to have with coffee, roll the biscuits out thinner and bake for 5–8 minutes.

Spritzgebäck Biscuits

These delicate, buttery biscuits are based on a classic German cookie traditionally served at Christmas. ▶

MAKES 45 | 45 MINS | 15 MINS

Special equipment
piping bag and star nozzle

Ingredients
380g (13oz) butter, softened
250g (9oz) caster sugar
few drops of vanilla extract
pinch of salt
500g (1lb 2oz) plain flour, sifted
125g (4½oz) ground almonds
2 egg yolks, if needed
100g (3½oz) dark or milk chocolate

Method
1 Preheat the oven to 180°C (350°F/Gas 4). Line 2–3 baking sheets with parchment. Place the butter in a bowl and beat until smooth. Stir in the sugar, vanilla, and salt until the mixture is thick, and the sugar has been absorbed. Gradually add two-thirds of the flour, stirring in a little at a time.

2 Add the rest of the flour and almonds, and knead the mixture to make a dough. Transfer the dough to the piping bag and squeeze 7.5cm (3in) lengths onto the baking sheets. Loosen the dough with 2 egg yolks, if necessary.

3 Bake for 12 minutes or until golden, and transfer to a wire rack. Melt the chocolate in a bowl over a pan of simmering water. Dip one end of the biscuits into the melted chocolate and return to the rack to set.

STORE The biscuits will keep in an airtight container for 2–3 days.

BISCUITS, COOKIES, AND SLICES

Gingerbread Men

All children love to make gingerbread men. This recipe is quick and the dough is easy for little bakers to handle.

MAKES 16 | 20 MINS | 10–12 MINS | 8 WEEKS, UNBAKED

Special equipment
11cm (4½in) gingerbread man cutter
piping bag with thin nozzle (optional)

Ingredients
4 tbsp golden syrup
300g (10½oz) plain flour,
 plus extra for dusting
1 tsp bicarbonate of soda
1½ tsp ground ginger
1½ tsp mixed spice
100g (3½oz) unsalted butter,
 softened and diced
150g (5½oz) soft dark brown sugar

1 egg
raisins, to decorate
icing sugar, sifted (optional)

BISCUITS, COOKIES, AND SLICES

1 Preheat the oven to 190°C (375°F/Gas 5). Heat the golden syrup till it liquefies, then cool.

2 Sift the flour, bicarbonate of soda, and spices into a bowl. Add the butter.

3 Rub together with your fingertips until the mixture looks like fine breadcrumbs.

4 Add the sugar to the breadcrumbs mixture and mix well.

5 Beat the egg into the cooled syrup until well blended.

6 Make a well in the flour mixture. Pour in the syrup mix. Bring together to a rough dough.

7 On a lightly floured work surface, knead the dough briefly until smooth.

8 Flour the dough and the work surface well, and roll the dough out to 5mm (¼in) thick.

9 Using the cutter, cut out as many shapes as possible. Transfer to non-stick baking sheets.

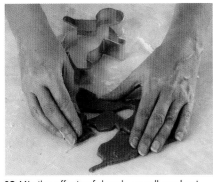

10 Mix the offcuts of dough, re-roll, and cut out more shapes until all the dough is used.

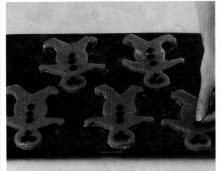

11 Decorate the men with raisins, giving them eyes, a nose, and buttons down the front.

12 Bake for 10–12 minutes until golden. Transfer to a wire rack to cool completely.

13 If using, mix a little icing sugar in a bowl with enough water to form a thin icing.

14 Transfer the icing into the piping bag; placing the bag into a jug first will help.

15 Decorate the men with the piped icing to resemble clothes, hair, or whatever you prefer.

16 Leave the icing to set completely before serving or storing. **STORE** These gingerbread men will keep in an airtight container for 3 days.

Gingerbread variations

Swedish Spice Biscuits

A version of the traditional Swedish Christmas biscuits. Roll them as thin as you dare (and bake for less time) for a truly authentic result.

MAKES 60	20 MINS	10 MINS	8 WEEKS, UNBAKED

Chilling time
1 hr

Special equipment
7cm (3in) heart or star-shaped pastry cutters

Ingredients
125g (4½oz) unsalted butter, softened
150g (5½oz) caster sugar
1 egg
1 tbsp golden syrup
1 tbsp black treacle
250g (9oz) plain flour, plus extra for dusting
pinch of salt
1 tsp cinnamon
1 tsp ground ginger
1 tsp mixed spice

Method
1 With an electric whisk, cream the butter and sugar. Beat in the egg, golden syrup, and black treacle. Sift together the flour, salt, and spices in a separate bowl. Add the flour mixture to the biscuit batter, and bring it all together to form a rough dough.

2 Briefly knead until smooth, place in a plastic bag and chill for 1 hour.

3 Preheat the oven to 180°C (350°F/Gas 4). Roll the dough out to a thickness of 3mm (⅛in) and cut out shapes with pastry cutters.

4 Transfer the biscuits to several non-stick baking sheets and bake in the top third of the oven for 10 minutes until the edges darken slightly. Leave on the trays for a few minutes, then transfer onto a wire rack to cool completely.

STORE The biscuits will keep in an airtight container for 5 days.

BAKER'S TIP

These are based on a Swedish Christmas biscuit called *Pepparkakor*. To decorate a Christmas tree in traditional Swedish style, cut the biscuits into heart shapes and use a straw to cut a hole out of the top before cooking. Once baked, tie the biscuits onto the tree using red ribbon.

Gingernut Biscuits

The addition of chopped nuts makes these biscuits extra special.

MAKES 45	30 MINS	8–10 MINS	8 WEEKS, UNBAKED

Special equipment
7cm (3in) pastry cutters (any shape)

Ingredients
250g (9oz) plain flour, plus extra for dusting
2 tsp baking powder
175g (6oz) caster sugar
few drops of vanilla extract
½ tsp mixed spice
2 tsp ground ginger
100g (3½oz) clear honey
1 egg, separated
4 tsp milk
125g (4½oz) butter, softened and diced
125g (4½oz) ground almonds
chopped hazelnuts or almonds, to decorate

Method
1 Preheat the oven to 180°C (350°F/Gas 4). Line 2 baking trays with baking parchment.

2 Sift the flour and baking powder into a bowl. Add all the other ingredients except the chopped nuts. With a wooden spoon, bring the mixture together to form a soft dough. Use your hands to shape the dough into a ball.

3 Roll the dough out on a lightly floured surface to 5mm (¼in) thickness. Cut out the biscuits with cutters, and place on the baking trays, spaced apart to allow them to spread. Beat the egg white and brush over the biscuits, then sprinkle over the nuts. Bake for 8–10 minutes or until lightly golden brown.

4 Remove from the oven and allow to cool on the tray for a few minutes, then transfer to a wire rack to cool completely.

STORE These gingernut biscuits will keep in an airtight container for 3 days.

BISCUITS, COOKIES, AND SLICES

Cinnamon Stars

These classic German cookies make a great last-minute Christmas gift.

| MAKES 30 | 20 MINS | 12–15 MINS | 4 WEEKS, UNBAKED |

Chilling time
1 hr

Special equipment
7cm (3in) star-shaped pastry cutter

Ingredients
2 large egg whites
225g (8oz) icing sugar, plus extra for dusting
½ tsp lemon juice
1 tsp cinnamon
250g (9oz) ground almonds
vegetable oil, for greasing
a little milk, if needed

Method

1 Whisk the egg whites until they are quite stiff. Sift in the icing sugar, add the lemon juice and continue to whisk for another 5 minutes, until thick and glossy. Take out 2 tablespoons of the mixture, cover and set aside for topping the cookies later.

2 Gently fold the cinnamon and ground almonds into the remaining mixture. Cover and refrigerate for 1 hour or overnight. The mixture will resemble a thick paste.

3 Preheat the oven to 160°C (325°F/Gas 3). Dust a work surface with icing sugar and turn the paste out onto it. Bring together with a little icing sugar to form a soft dough. Dust a rolling pin with icing sugar and roll out the dough to 5mm (¼in) thick.

4 Oil the cutter and non-stick baking sheets. Cut star shapes out of the dough. Lay the cookies on the sheets. Brush a little of the meringue mix over the surface of each cookie, mixing it with a little milk, if too thick.

5 Bake in the top third of the oven for 12–15 minutes until the topping has set. Leave to cool for at least 10 minutes on the baking sheets, then transfer to a wire rack.

STORE The biscuits will keep in an airtight container for 5 days.

Canestrelli

These delightful Italian biscuits are as light as air and traditionally made with a flower-shaped cutter – a fitting shape for such a delicate biscuit.

MAKES 20–30 | **20 MINS** | **15–20 MINS** | **UP TO 4 WEEKS**

Chilling time
30 mins

Special equipment
flower-shaped pastry cutter,
or 2 different-sized round cutters

Ingredients

3 egg yolks, unbroken
150g (5½oz) unsalted butter, softened
150g (5½oz) icing sugar, sifted
finely grated zest of ½ lemon
150g (5½oz) potato flour
100g (3½oz) self-raising flour
  (or more potato flour if you are wheat
  intolerant), plus extra for dusting

Method

1 Gently slide the egg yolks into a pan of simmering water over low heat. Poach for 5 minutes, until completely hard, then take them out of the water and set aside to cool. When they are cool, push the egg yolks through a fine metal sieve with the back of a spoon. Scrape into a small bowl.

2 Cream together the butter and icing sugar with an electric whisk until light and fluffy. Add the egg yolks and lemon zest, and beat well to combine.

3 Sift the flours together and add to the biscuit batter, beating well to form a smooth, soft dough. Place the dough in a plastic bag and refrigerate for 30 minutes to firm up. Preheat the oven to 160°C (325°F/Gas 3) and have 3 or 4 non-stick baking sheets ready.

4 Roll out the chilled dough on a lightly floured work surface to 1cm (½in) thick. Cut out traditional flower-shaped cookies, or other shapes. If you do not have a flower-shaped cutter, use a larger and a smaller cutter to make ring shapes instead.

5 Place the cookies on the baking sheets and bake in the top third of the oven for 15–17 minutes until just turning golden. The canestrelli are very delicate when warm, so leave them to cool for at least 10 minutes on their baking sheets before removing to a wire rack to cool completely.

STORE The canestrelli will keep in an airtight container for 5 days.

BAKER'S TIP

These delicate biscuits originate from the Liguria region of Italy. Their light texture comes from the traditional use of potato flour in the recipe. If you cannot find any potato flour, an "00" grade flour (from larger supermarkets and Italian delicatessens), or even plain flour, will make a good substitute.

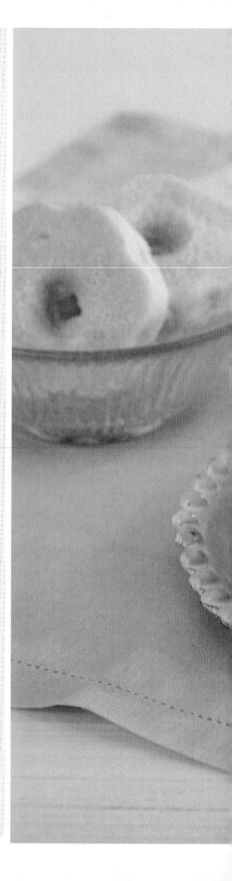

Macaroons

These almond meringue biscuits (not to be confused with French macarons) are crisp outside and chewy inside.

MAKES 24 | 10 MINS | 12–15 MINS

Special equipment
sheets of edible wafer paper (optional)

Ingredients
2 egg whites
225g (8oz) caster sugar
125g (4½oz) ground almonds
30g (1oz) rice flour
a few drops of almond extract
24 blanched almonds

1 Preheat the oven to 180°C (350°F/Gas 4). Use an electric whisk to stiffen the egg whites.

2 Gradually whisk in the sugar, a tablespoon at a time, to give a thick, glossy meringue.

3 Fold in the ground almonds, rice flour, and almond extract until well combined.

4 Divide the wafer paper, if using, between 2 baking sheets, or line them with parchment.

5 Use 2 teaspoons to scoop and shape the mixture, cleaning and drying between scoops.

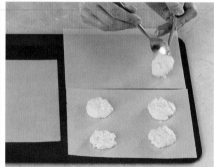

6 Place 4 teaspoons of mixture, spaced apart, on each piece of edible wafer paper.

7 Keep the mixture in rounds. Put a blanched almond in the centre of each biscuit.

8 Bake the macaroons in the centre of the oven for 12–15 minutes or until lightly golden.

9 Transfer to a wire rack to cool completely, before tearing each biscuit from the paper.

Macaroons are prone to sticking, but by using edible wafer it doesn't matter if the paper tears off with the biscuit. **STORE** Macaroons are best eaten on the day they are made. They will keep for 2–3 days in an airtight container, but tend to dry out.

Macaroon variations

Coconut Macaroons

Coconut macaroons are simple to make and completely wheat-free. I've omitted chocolate from my version so that they remain a light treat.

MAKES 18–20	20 MINS	15–20 MINS

Chilling time
2 hrs

Special equipment
sheets of edible wafer paper (optional)

Ingredients
1 egg white
50g (1¾oz) caster sugar
pinch of salt
½ tsp vanilla extract
100g (3½oz) desiccated,
  or sweetened shredded, coconut

Method

1 Preheat the oven to 160°C (325°F/Gas 3). In a large bowl, beat the egg whites with an electric whisk until stiff. Add the sugar a little at a time, whisking between each addition, until all the sugar is combined and the mixture is thick and glossy.

2 Add the salt and vanilla extract, and briefly whisk again to blend.

3 Gently fold in the coconut. Cover and refrigerate for 2 hours to firm up. This will also allow the desiccated coconut to hydrate and soften.

4 Line a baking sheet with parchment or wafer paper (if using). Place heaped teaspoons of the mixture onto the baking sheet; try to keep each portion of the mixture in a small heap.

5 Bake in the middle of the oven for 15–20 minutes until golden brown in places. Leave the macaroons to cool on the trays for at least 10 minutes to firm up, then transfer to a wire rack to cool completely.

STORE The macaroons will keep in an airtight container for 5 days.

Chocolate Macaroons

Add cocoa powder for a chocolate version of the basic macaroon.

MAKES 24	20 MINS	15 MINS	UP TO 4 WEEKS

Chilling time
30 mins

Special equipment
sheets of edible wafer paper (optional)

Ingredients
2 egg whites
225g (8oz) caster sugar
100g (3½oz) ground almonds
30g (1oz) rice flour
25g (scant 1oz) cocoa powder, sifted
24 whole blanched almonds

Method

1 Preheat the oven to 180°C (350°F/Gas 4). In a large bowl, beat the egg whites with an electric whisk, until stiff. Add the sugar a little at a time, whisking between each addition, until all the sugar is combined and the mixture is thick and glossy.

2 Fold in the almonds, rice flour, and then the cocoa powder. Cover and refrigerate for 30 minutes to firm up. Line 2 baking sheets with parchment or wafer paper (if using).

3 Place heaped teaspoons of the mixture onto the prepared baking sheets, spacing them at least 4cm (1½in) apart as they will spread. Try to keep each portion of the mixture in a small heap. Place a blanched almond in the centre of each heap.

4 Bake the macaroons at the top of the oven for 12–15 minutes until the exterior is crisp and the edges firm to the touch. Leave the macaroons to cool on the sheets for at least 5 minutes, then transfer to a wire rack to cool completely.

STORE Best eaten on the day, these will keep in an airtight container for 2–3 days.

Coffee and Hazelnut Macaroons

These gorgeous little biscuits are easy to prepare, infused with flavour, and look very pretty served after dinner with coffee, especially if you make them on the smaller side.

MAKES 20 | **30 MINS** | **20 MINS** | **UP TO 4 WEEKS**

Chilling time
30 mins

Special equipment
food processor with blade attachment
sheets of edible wafer paper (optional)

Ingredients
150g (5½oz) hazelnuts, shelled, plus 20 extra
2 egg whites
225g (8oz) caster sugar
30g (1oz) rice flour
1 tsp strong instant coffee powder, dissolved in 1 tsp boiling water and cooled, or equivalent cooled espresso

Method

1 Preheat the oven to 180°C (350°F/Gas 4). Place the hazelnuts on a baking tray and toast for 5 minutes. Put them in a tea towel and rub to remove skin. Set aside to cool.

2 Whisk the egg whites until stiff. Add the sugar a little at a time, whisking, until all the sugar is combined and the mixture is thick.

3 In a food processor, blitz the hazelnuts to a powder. Fold them into the meringue mixture with the rice flour, and gently fold in a teaspoon of the coffee mixture. Cover and refrigerate for 30 minutes to firm up.

4 Place teaspoons of the mixture onto baking sheets lined with parchment or wafer paper, spacing them at least 4cm (1½in) apart. Keep each portion in a small heap and place a whole hazelnut in the centre.

5 Bake the macaroons at the top of the oven for 12–15 minutes, until crisp and colouring slightly; check after 10 minutes if making them small. Leave on the trays for 5 minutes and transfer to a wire rack to cool.

STORE Best eaten on the day, these will keep in an airtight container for 2–3 days.

BAKER'S TIP
Old-fashioned macaroons have been rather overshadowed of late by their prettier French cousins, macarons (see pages 158–163). However, macaroons are also wheat-free, easier to make, and just as pretty, in an understated kind of way.

Strawberries and Cream Macarons

The art of macaron making can seem complex, but here I have tried to devise a recipe that will suit the home cook.

MAKES 20 | 30 MINS | 18–20 MINS

Special equipment
food processor with
  blade attachment
piping bag with small,
  plain nozzle

Ingredients
100g (3½oz) icing sugar
75g (2½oz) ground almonds
2 large egg whites,
  at room temperature
75g (2½oz) granulated sugar

For the filling
200ml (7fl oz) double cream
5–10 very large strawberries,
  preferably the same diameter
  as the macarons

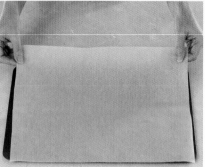

1 Preheat the oven to 150°C (300°F/Gas 2). Line 2 baking sheets with silicone paper.

2 Trace 20 x 3cm (1¼in) circles, leaving 3cm (1¼in) between circles. Invert the paper.

3 In a food processor, whizz together the almonds and icing sugar to a very fine meal.

4 In a large bowl, whisk the egg whites to stiff peaks using an electric whisk.

5 Whisking, add the granulated sugar a little at a time, whisking well between additions.

6 The meringue mixture should be very stiff at this point, more than for a Swiss meringue.

7 Gently fold in the almond mixture a spoonful at a time, until just incorporated.

8 Transfer the macaron mix to the piping bag, placing the bag into a bowl to help.

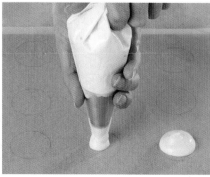

9 Using the guidelines, pipe the mix into the centre of each circle, holding the bag vertically.

10 Try to keep the disks even in size and volume; the mix will spread only very slightly.

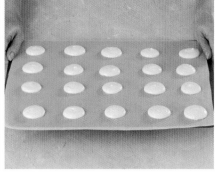

11 Bang the baking sheets down a few times if there are any peaks left in the centre.

12 Bake in the middle of the oven for 18–20 minutes until the surface is set firm.

13 Test one shell: a firm prod with a finger should crack the top of the macaron.

14 Leave for 15–20 minutes, then transfer to a wire rack to cool completely.

15 Whisk the cream until thick; a soft whip would ooze out the sides and soften the shells.

16 Transfer the cream into the (cleaned) piping bag used earlier, with the same nozzle.

17 Pipe a blob of the whipped cream onto the flat side of half the macarons.

18 Slice the strawberries widthways into thin slices, the same diameter as the macarons.

19 Put a slice of strawberry on top of the cream filling of each macaron.

20 Add the remaining macaron shells and sandwich gently. The fillings should peek out.

21 Serve immediately. **PREPARE AHEAD** Unfilled macaron shells can be stored for 3 days.

Macaron variations

Tangerine Macarons

Sharp, zesty tangerines are used here, rather than the more usual oranges, to counter-balance the sweetness of the meringues.

MAKES 20 | 30 MINS | 18–20 MINS

Special equipment
food processor with blade attachment

Ingredients
100g (3½oz) icing sugar
75g (2½oz) ground almonds
1 scant tsp finely grated tangerine zest
2 large egg whites, at room temperature
75g (2½oz) granulated sugar
3–4 drops orange food colouring

For the filling
100g (3½oz) icing sugar
50g (1¾oz) unsalted butter, softened
1 tbsp tangerine juice
1 scant tsp finely grated tangerine zest

Method
1 Preheat the oven to 150°C (300°F/Gas 2). Line 2 baking sheets with silicone paper. Draw on 3cm (1¼in) circles with a pencil, leaving 3cm (1¼in) gap between each one. Whizz the icing sugar and ground almonds in a food processor, until finely mixed. Add the tangerine zest and whizz briefly.

2 In a bowl, whisk the egg whites to form stiff peaks. Add the granulated sugar a little at a time, whisking well with each addition. Whisk in the food colouring.

3 Fold in the almond mixture, a spoonful at a time. Transfer to the piping bag. Holding the bag vertically, pipe meringue into the centre of each circle.

4 Bake in the middle of the oven for 18–20 minutes until the surface is set firm. Leave the macarons to cool on the baking sheets for 15–20 minutes and then transfer to a wire rack to cool completely.

5 For the filling, cream together the icing sugar, butter, tangerine zest, and juice until smooth. Transfer into the (cleaned) piping bag, using the same nozzle. Pipe a blob of icing onto the flat side of half the macarons, and sandwich with the rest. Serve the same day, or the macarons will start to go soft.

PREPARE AHEAD The unfilled shells can be stored for 3 days in an airtight container.

Chocolate Macarons

These delicious macarons are filled with a rich, dark chocolate buttercream.

MAKES 20 | 30 MINS | 18–20 MINS

Special equipment
food processor with blade attachment

Ingredients
50g (1¾oz) ground almonds
25g (scant 1oz) cocoa powder
100g (3½oz) icing sugar
2 large egg whites, at room temperature
75g (2½oz) granulated sugar

For the filling
50g (1¾oz) cocoa powder
150g (5½oz) icing sugar
50g (1¾oz) unsalted butter, melted
3 tbsp milk, plus a little extra if needed

Method
1 Preheat the oven to 150°C (300°F/Gas 2). Line 2 baking sheets with silicone paper. Draw on 3cm (1¼in) circles with a pencil, leaving 3cm (1¼in) gap between each. In a food processor, whizz the ground almonds, cocoa, and icing sugar until mixed.

2 Whisk the egg whites until stiff. Add the granulated sugar, whisking. The mixture should be stiff. Fold in the almond mixture a spoonful at a time. Transfer to the piping bag. Holding the bag vertically, pipe meringue into the centre of each circle.

3 Bake in the middle of the oven for 18–20 minutes. Leave to cool on the sheets 15–20 minutes, before transferring to a wire rack.

4 For the filling, sift the cocoa and icing sugar into a bowl. Add the butter and milk, and whisk. Add a little milk if is too thick. Transfer into the piping bag and pipe icing onto the flat side of half the macarons, and sandwich together with the rest. Serve the same day, or the macarons will go soft.

PREPARE AHEAD The unfilled shells can be stored for 3 days in an airtight container.

Raspberry Macarons

Pretty as a picture, these macarons look almost too good to eat.

MAKES 20 · 30 MINS · 18–20 MINS

Special equipment
food processor with blade attachment

Ingredients
100g (3½oz) icing sugar
75g (2½oz) ground almonds
2 large egg whites, at room temperature
75g (2½oz) granulated sugar
3–4 drops of pink food colouring

For the filling
150g (5½oz) mascarpone
50g (1¾oz) seedless raspberry conserve

Method

1 Preheat the oven to 150°C (300°F/Gas 2). Line 2 baking sheets with silicone paper. Draw on 3cm (1¼in) circles with a pencil, leaving 3cm (1¼in) gap between each. In a food processor, whizz together the icing sugar and ground almonds until very finely mixed and smooth.

2 In a bowl, whisk the egg whites until they form stiff peaks. Add the granulated sugar, a little at a time, whisking well between each addition. Whisk in the food colouring.

3 Fold in the almond mixture a spoonful at a time, until just mixed. Transfer the mix to the piping bag. Holding the bag vertically, pipe meringue into the centre of each circle.

4 Bake in the middle of the oven for 18–20 minutes until the surface is firm. Leave to cool on the sheets for 15–20 minutes, before transferring to a wire rack to cool.

5 For the filling, beat the mascarpone and raspberry conserve until smooth and transfer to the (cleaned) piping bag used earlier, with the same nozzle. Pipe a blob of the filling onto the flat side of half the macarons, and sandwich together with the rest of the halves. Serve the same day, or the macarons will go soft.

PREPARE AHEAD The unfilled shells can be stored for 3 days in an airtight container.

BAKER'S TIP
The skill in making macarons comes in the technique, not in the proportions of the ingredients. Gentle folding, a heavy, flat baking sheet, and piping the mix completely vertically downwards should all help to produce the perfect macaron.

Vanillekipferl

These crescent-shaped German biscuits are often served at the same time as Cinnamon Stars (see page 151), making a truly festive platter.

MAKES 30	35 MINS	15–17 MINS	UP TO 4 WEEKS

Chilling time
30 mins

Ingredients
200g (7oz) plain flour, plus extra for dusting
150g (5½oz) unsalted butter, softened and diced
75g (2½oz) icing sugar
75g (2½oz) ground almonds
1 tsp vanilla extract
1 egg, beaten
vanilla sugar or icing sugar, to serve

Method

1 Sift the flour into a large bowl. Rub in the softened butter until the mixture resembles fine crumbs. Sift in the icing sugar, and add the ground almonds.

2 Add the vanilla extract to the egg, then pour it into the flour mixture. Bring the mixture together to form a soft dough, adding a little more flour if the mixture is very sticky. Place the dough in a plastic bag and chill it for at least 30 minutes until firm.

3 Preheat the oven to 160°C (325°F/Gas 3). Divide the dough into 2 parts, and on a lightly floured work surface, roll each part into a sausage shape, approximately 3cm (1½in) in diameter. Use a sharp knife to cut 1cm (½in) pieces from the dough.

4 To form the cookies, take a piece of the dough and roll it between your palms to make a sausage shape of around 8 x 2cm (3½–¾in), tapering it slightly at each end.

Fold each end of the roll in slightly to form a crescent shape. Line 2 baking sheets with baking parchment, and place the formed cookies on them, leaving a little space between each.

5 Bake the vanillekipferl at the top of the oven for 15 minutes until they are very lightly coloured. They should not brown at all.

6 Leave the cookies to cool on their trays for 5 minutes, then either toss in vanilla sugar or liberally dust with icing sugar and transfer to a wire rack to cool completely.

STORE The vanillekipferl will keep in an airtight container for 5 days.

BAKER'S TIP

A German Christmas tradition, these crescent-shaped biscuits rely on the use of ground almonds for their delicate, crumbly texture. Many recipes recommend tossing the finished biscuits in vanilla sugar, but if that proves difficult to find, the vanilla extract in the biscuit dough will do just as well.

Florentines

These crisp Italian biscuits are packed full of fruit and nuts, and coated with luxurious dark chocolate – wonderful for a quick teatime treat.

| MAKES 16–20 | 20 MINS | 15–20 MINS |

Ingredients
60g (2oz) butter
60g (2oz) caster sugar
1 tbsp clear honey

60g (2oz) plain flour, sifted
45g (1½oz) chopped mixed peel
45g (1½oz) glacé cherries, finely chopped
45g (1½oz) blanched almonds, finely chopped
1 tsp lemon juice
1 tbsp double cream
175g (6oz) good-quality dark chocolate,
  broken into pieces

Method

1 Preheat the oven to 180°C (350°F/Gas 4) and line 2 baking sheets with parchment.

2 Put the butter, sugar, and honey into a small saucepan, and melt gently over low heat. Allow it to cool until it is just warm. Stir in all the other ingredients except the chocolate.

3 Using a teaspoon, drop spoonfuls of the mixture onto the baking sheets, leaving space between them for the biscuits to spread.

4 Bake for 10 minutes or until golden. Do not let them get too dark. Leave them on the baking sheets for a few minutes, before lifting them onto a wire rack to cool completely.

5 Put the chocolate pieces into a heatproof bowl set over a pan of gently simmering water. Make sure the bowl is not touching the water.

6 Once the chocolate has melted, use a palette knife to spread a thin layer of chocolate on the bottom of each biscuit. Place the biscuits chocolate-side up on a wire rack to set. Spread a second layer of chocolate over the biscuits, then just before it sets, make a wavy line in the chocolate with a fork.

STORE The Florentines will keep in an airtight container for 5 days.

BAKER'S TIP
You can make a beautiful display of three different colours of Florentines by topping one-third with milk chocolate, another third with white chocolate, and the remainder with dark chocolate. Or use different tones of chocolate both to top and to drizzle over in a zigzag fashion, for an impressive effect.

Biscotti

These crisp Italian biscuits make great presents, as they can be prettily packaged and will keep for days.

MAKES 25–30 | 15 MINS | 40–45 MINS | UP TO 8 WEEKS

Ingredients

50g (1¾oz) unsalted butter
100g (3½oz) whole almonds,
  shelled and skinned
225g (8oz) self-raising flour,
  plus extra for dusting
100g (3½oz) caster sugar
2 eggs
1 tsp vanilla extract

1 Melt the butter in small pan over low heat and then set aside to cool.

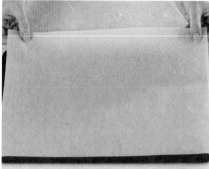

2 Preheat the oven to 180°C (350°F/Gas 4). Line a baking sheet with parchment.

3 Spread the almonds out on a non-stick baking sheet. Place in the centre of the oven.

4 Bake the almonds for 5–10 minutes until slightly coloured, tossing halfway.

5 Allow the almonds to cool until they are comfortable to handle and roughly chop them.

6 Sift the flour through a fine sieve held over a large bowl.

7 Add the sugar and chopped almonds to the bowl and stir until well combined.

8 In a separate bowl, whisk together the eggs, vanilla extract, and the melted butter.

9 Gradually pour the egg mixture into the flour, while stirring with a fork.

10 Using your hands, bring the ingredients together to form a dough.

11 If the mixture seems too wet to shape easily, work in a little flour until it is pliable.

12 Turn the dough out onto a lightly floured work surface.

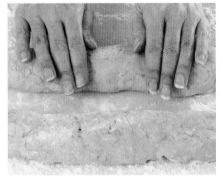

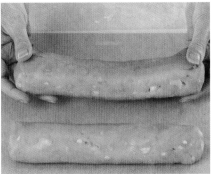

13 With your hands, form the dough into 2 log shapes, each about 20cm (8in) long.

14 Place on the lined baking sheet and bake for 20 minutes in the middle of the oven.

15 Remove the logs from the oven. Cool slightly, then transfer to a chopping board.

16 With a serrated knife, cut the logs on a slant into 3–5cm (1½–2in) thick slices.

17 Put the biscotti on a baking sheet and return to the oven for 10 minutes to dry even more.

18 Turn the biscotti with a palette knife, and return to the oven for another 5 minutes.

19 Cool the biscotti on a wire rack to harden them and allow any moisture to escape.

TO FREEZE Place the cooled biscotti on baking sheets and freeze till solid.

Transfer to freezer bags. **STORE** Keep unfrozen in an airtight container for over 1 week.

Biscotti variations

Hazelnut and Chocolate Biscotti

Add chocolate chips to the biscotti dough for a child-friendly alternative.

MAKES 25–30 | **15 MINS** | **40–45 MINS** | **UP TO 8 WEEKS**

Ingredients
100g (3½oz) whole hazelnuts, shelled
225g (8oz) self-raising flour, sifted,
  plus extra for dusting
100g (3½oz) caster sugar
50g (1¾oz) dark chocolate chips
2 eggs
1 tsp vanilla extract
50g (1¾oz) unsalted butter, melted and cooled

Method
1 Preheat the oven to 180°C (350°F/Gas 4). Line a baking sheet with silicone paper. Spread the hazelnuts out on an unlined baking sheet and bake for 5–10 minutes, tossing halfway through, until slightly coloured. Allow to cool, rub in a tea towel to remove excess skin, then roughly chop.

2 In a bowl, mix together the flour, sugar, nuts, and chocolate chips. In a separate bowl, whisk together the eggs, vanilla extract, and butter. Combine the wet and dry ingredients, working them together to form a dough. If the mixture is too wet, knead in a little extra flour to shape easily.

3 Turn the dough out onto a floured surface and form into 2 logs, each 20cm (8in) long by 7cm (3in). Place on the lined baking sheet and bake for 20 minutes in the middle of the oven. Take the biscotti logs out of the oven, allow them to cool slightly. Cut them diagonally into 3–5cm (1¼–2in) thick slices with a serrated knife.

4 Return the sliced biscotti to the oven for another 15 minutes, turning them after 10 minutes. They are ready when golden at the edges and hard to the touch. Cool on a wire rack.

STORE These will keep in an airtight container for more than 1 week.

Chocolate and Brazil Nut Biscotti

These biscotti, darkened with cocoa powder, are ideal to serve after dinner with strong, black coffee.

MAKES 25–30 | **15 MINS** | **40–45 MINS** | **UP TO 8 WEEKS**

Ingredients
100g (3½oz) whole Brazil nuts, shelled
175g (6oz) self-raising flour, sifted,
  plus extra for dusting
50g (1¾oz) cocoa powder
100g (3½oz) caster sugar
2 eggs
1 tsp vanilla extract
50g (1¾oz) unsalted butter, melted and cooled

Method
1 Preheat the oven to 180°C (350°F/Gas 4). Line a baking sheet with silicone paper. Spread the nuts on an unlined baking sheet and bake for 5–10 minutes. Allow them to cool slightly, rub in a clean tea towel to remove excess skin, then roughly chop.

2 In a bowl, mix together the flour, cocoa powder, sugar, and nuts. In a separate bowl, whisk together the eggs, vanilla extract, and butter. Combine the wet and dry ingredients together to form a dough.

3 Turn the dough out onto a floured surface and form into 2 logs, each 20cm (8in) long by 7cm (3in). Place on the lined baking sheet and bake for 20 minutes. Cool slightly, then cut them diagonally into 3–5cm (1¼–2in) thick slices with a serrated knife.

4 Return to the oven for 15 minutes, turning after 10, until golden and hard to the touch.

STORE These will keep in an airtight container for more than 1 week.

BAKER'S TIP
The hard, crunchy texture and toasted taste of biscotti is obtained by double-baking. This technique also allows them to keep well for a relatively long time.

Pistachio and Orange Biscotti

These fragrant biscotti are delicious served either with coffee or dipped in a glass of sweet dessert wine. ▶

MAKES 25–30 | **15 MINS** | **40–45 MINS** | **UP TO 8 WEEKS**

Ingredients
100g (3½oz) whole pistachios, shelled
225g (8oz) self-raising flour,
  plus extra for dusting
100g (3½oz) caster sugar
finely grated zest of 1 orange
2 eggs
1 tsp vanilla extract
50g (1¾oz) unsalted butter, melted and cooled

Method
1 Preheat the oven to 180°C (350°F/Gas 4). Spread the pistachios on an unlined baking sheet. Bake for 5–10 minutes. Allow to cool, rub in a clean tea towel to remove excess skin, then roughly chop.

2 In a bowl, mix the flour, sugar, zest, and nuts. In a separate bowl, whisk together the eggs, vanilla extract, and butter. Mix the wet and dry ingredients to form a dough.

3 Turn the dough out onto a floured surface and form into 2 logs, each 20cm (8in) long by 7cm (3in). Place them on a baking sheet lined with silicone paper and bake for 20 minutes in the centre of the oven. Cool slightly, then cut diagonally into 3–5cm (1¼–2in) thick slices with a serrated knife.

4 Bake for another 15 minutes, turning after 10, until golden and hard to the touch.

STORE These will keep in an airtight container for more than 1 week.

Shortbread

A Scottish classic, shortbread should only colour very lightly in the oven, so remember to cover with foil if browning.

MAKES 8 WEDGES | **15 MINS** | **30–40 MINS**

Chilling time
1 hr

Special equipment
18cm (7in) loose-bottomed
  round cake tin

Ingredients
150g (5½oz) unsalted butter,
  softened, plus extra for greasing
75g (2½oz) caster sugar,
  plus extra for sprinkling

175g (6oz) plain flour
50g (1¾oz) cornflour

1 Preheat the oven to 160°C (325°F/Gas 3). Grease the tin and line with parchment.

2 Place the softened butter and sugar in a large bowl.

3 Cream together the butter and sugar with an electric whisk until light and fluffy.

4 Stir in the flour and cornflour very gently, stopping as soon as the flours are mixed in.

5 Bring together with your hands to form a very rough, crumbly dough. Transfer to the tin.

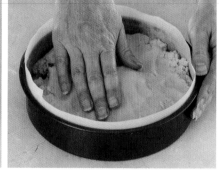

6 Firmly push the dough down with your hands to form a compact, even layer.

7 With a sharp knife, lightly score the circle of shortbread into 8 wedges.

8 Prick the shortbread all over with a fork to make a decorative pattern.

9 Cover the shortbread with cling film and chill in the refrigerator for 1 hour.

BISCUITS, COOKIES, AND SLICES

10 Bake in the centre of the oven for 30–40 minutes. Cover with foil if it browns quickly.

11 Take the shortbread out of the oven, and re-score the wedges with a sharp knife.

12 While it is still warm, sprinkle a thin layer of caster sugar evenly over the top.

13 When completely cool, turn the shortbread gently out of its tin and break or cut it into wedges along the scored lines.

STORE The shortbread will keep in an airtight container for up to 5 days.

Shortbread variations

Pecan Sandies

These addictive shortbread cookies are so-called because they are said to have the texture (though not the taste!) of fine sand.

MAKES 18–20 **15 MINS** **15 MINS**

Chilling time
30 mins (if needed)

Ingredients
100g (3½oz) unsalted butter, softened
50g (1¾oz) soft light brown sugar
50g (1¾oz) caster sugar
½ tsp vanilla extract
1 egg yolk
150g (5½oz) plain flour, sifted,
  plus extra for dusting
75g (2½oz) pecan nuts, chopped

Method
1 Preheat the oven to 180°C (350°F/Gas 4). In a large bowl, cream together the butter and sugars with an electric whisk, until light and fluffy. Add the vanilla extract and the egg yolk, and mix well to combine. Fold in the flour and then the pecans. Bring the ingredients together to form a rough dough.

2 Turn the dough out onto a lightly floured work surface and knead it to form a smooth dough. Roll into a log about 20cm (8in) long. If the dough seems too soft to cut, refrigerate it for 30 minutes to allow it to firm up.

3 Slice 1cm (½in) disks from the log, and place a little apart on 2 baking sheets lined with baking parchment. Bake in the top third of the oven for 15 minutes until golden brown at the edges. Leave on the sheets for a few minutes, then transfer them to a wire rack to cool completely.

STORE The sandies will keep in an airtight container for 5 days.

Chocolate Chip Shortbread Cookies

Chocolate chips make these shortbread cookies child-friendly.

MAKES 14–16 **15 MINS** **15–20 MINS**

Ingredients
100g (3½oz) unsalted butter, softened
75g (2½oz) caster sugar
100g (3½oz) plain flour, sifted,
  plus extra for dusting
25g (scant 1oz) cornflour, sifted
50g (1¾oz) dark chocolate chips

Method
1 Preheat the oven to 170°C (340°F/Gas 3½). In a large bowl, cream together the butter and sugar with an electric whisk, until light and fluffy. Stir in the flour, cornflour, and chocolate chips, and bring together to form a rough dough.

2 Turn the dough out onto a lightly floured work surface and gently knead it until it becomes smooth. Roll into a 6cm (2½in) diameter log, and slice at 5mm (¼in) intervals into biscuits. Place a little apart on 2 non-stick baking sheets.

3 Bake in the centre of the oven for about 15–20 minutes until lightly golden. They should not colour too much. Leave on the sheets for a few minutes before transferring to a wire rack to cool completely.

STORE The cookies will keep in an airtight container for 5 days.

Marbled Millionaire's Shortbread

A modern classic – extremely sweet and rich, just as it should be.

MAKES 16 SQUARES | **45 MINS** | **35–40 MINS**

Special equipment
20cm (8in) square cake tin

Ingredients
200g (7oz) plain flour
175g (6oz) unsalted butter, softened,
 plus extra for greasing
100g (3½oz) caster sugar

For the caramel filling
50g (1¾oz) unsalted butter
50g (1¾oz) light brown sugar
400g can condensed milk

For the chocolate topping
200g (7oz) milk chocolate
25g (scant 1oz) unsalted butter
50g (1¾oz) dark chocolate

Method

1 Preheat the oven to 160°C (325°F/Gas 3). Put the flour, butter, and sugar in a bowl and rub together to make crumbs. Grease the tin and line with parchment. Tip the mixture into the tin and press it down well with your hands until it is compact and even. Bake in the centre of the oven for 35–40 minutes until golden brown. Leave to cool in the tin.

2 For the caramel, melt the butter and sugar in a heavy saucepan over medium heat. Add the condensed milk and bring to a boil, stirring constantly. Reduce the heat and cook on a steady simmer, still stirring constantly, for 5 minutes until it thickens and darkens to a light caramel colour. Pour the caramel over the cooled shortbread and leave to cool.

3 To make the chocolate topping, place the milk chocolate and butter in a heatproof bowl over a pan of simmering water until just melted, stirring until smooth. Melt the dark chocolate without butter in a separate bowl set over simmering water.

4 Pour the milk chocolate over the set caramel and smooth out. Pour the dark chocolate over the surface in a zigzag pattern and drag a fine skewer through both the chocolates to create a marbled effect. Leave to cool and harden before cutting into squares.

STORE The shortbread will keep in an airtight container for 5 days.

BAKER'S TIP
The secret to a good millionaire's shortbread is to make a caramel that sets enough so that it does not squish out of the sides on cutting, and a chocolate topping that cuts easily. Adding butter to the chocolate softens it, and cooking the caramel until thickened will help achieve a perfect result.

Flapjacks

These chewy bars are great energy boosters and very simple to make, using only a few storecupboard ingredients.

MAKES 16–20   **15 MINS**   **40 MINS**

Special equipment
25cm (10in) square
cake tin

Ingredients
225g (8oz) butter,
  plus extra for greasing
225g (8oz) light soft brown sugar
2 tbsp golden syrup
350g (12oz) rolled oats

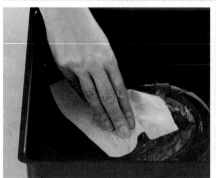

1 Preheat the oven to 150°C (300°F/Gas 2). Lightly grease the base and sides of the tin.

2 Put the butter, sugar, and syrup in a large saucepan and place over medium-low heat.

3 Stir constantly with a wooden spoon to prevent scorching. Remove from the heat.

4 Stir in the oats, making sure they are well coated, but do not over-work the mix.

5 Spoon the oat mixture from the saucepan into the prepared tin.

6 Press down firmly with the wooden spoon to make a roughly even layer.

7 To neaten the surface, dip a tablespoon in hot water and use the back to smooth the top.

8 Bake for 40 minutes or until evenly golden; you may need to turn the tin in the oven.

9 Leave to cool for 10 minutes, then cut into 16 squares, or 20 rectangles, with a sharp knife.

BISCUITS, COOKIES, AND SLICES

10 Leave in the tin to cool completely, then lever the flapjacks out of the tin; a fish slice is a useful tool for this.
STORE These will keep in an airtight container for 1 week.

Flapjack variations

Hazelnut and Raisin Flapjacks

Hazelnuts and raisins make these a chewy and wholesome treat.

MAKES 16–20 | **15 MINS** | **30 MINS** | **UP TO 4 WEEKS**

Special equipment
20 x 25cm (8 x 10in) brownie tin, or similar

Ingredients
225g (8oz) unsalted butter,
  plus extra for greasing
225g (8oz) soft light brown sugar
2 tbsp golden syrup
350g (12oz) rolled oats
75g (2½oz) chopped hazelnuts
50g (1¾oz) raisins

Method
1 Preheat the oven to 160°C (325°F/Gas 3). Grease the tin, and line the base and sides with baking parchment. Melt the butter, sugar, and syrup in a heavy saucepan over low heat until the butter has melted. Remove the pan from the heat and stir in the oats, hazelnuts, and raisins.

2 Transfer the mixture to the prepared tin and press it down firmly, until it is compact and even. Bake in the centre of the oven for 30 minutes until golden brown and darkening slightly at the edges.

3 Leave in the tin for 5 minutes, then cut the flapjacks into squares with a sharp knife. Leave in the tin until cold before turning out with a fish slice.

STORE The flapjacks can be kept in an airtight container for 1 week.

BAKER'S TIP
Nuts and raisins make these flapjacks healthier and, as in the recipes for Oat Cookies (see pages 140–142), you could also add a handful of pumpkin or sunflower seeds. Despite the health quotient of those ingredients, the butter content of flapjacks does make them a high-fat treat.

Cherry Flapjacks

Use dried cherries here for an unusual alternative to the more common dried fruits such as raisins and sultanas. ▶

MAKES 18 | **15 MINS** | **25 MINS**

Chilling time
10 mins

Special equipment
20cm (8in) square cake tin

Ingredients
150g (5½oz) unsalted butter,
  plus extra for greasing
75g (2½oz) light soft brown sugar
2 tbsp golden syrup
350g (12oz) rolled oats
125g (4½oz) glacé cherries, quartered, or
  75g (2½oz) dried cherries, roughly chopped
50g (1¾oz) raisins
100g (3½oz) white or milk chocolate,
  broken into small pieces, for drizzling

Method
1 Preheat the oven to 180°C (350°F/Gas 4). Lightly grease the cake tin. Place the butter, sugar, and syrup in a medium saucepan over low heat, and stir until melted. Remove from the heat, add the oats, cherries, and raisins, and stir until well mixed.

2 Transfer to the prepared tin and press down. Bake at the top of the oven for 25 minutes. Remove, cool slightly in the tin, then cut into 18 pieces with a knife.

3 When the flapjacks are cold, place the chocolate in a small heatproof bowl set over a saucepan of simmering water. Make sure the bowl does not touch the water, and leave the chocolate to melt. Drizzle the melted chocolate over the flapjacks using a teaspoon, then chill for 10 minutes or until the chocolate has set. Remove the flapjacks from the tin with a fish slice.

STORE The flapjacks can be kept in an airtight container for 1 week.

Sticky Date Flapjacks

The quantity of dates in this recipe gives these flapjacks a toffee-like flavour and wonderfully moist consistency.

MAKES 16 | **25 MINS** | **40 MINS**

Special equipment
20cm (8in) square cake tin
blender

Ingredients
200g (7oz) stoned dates, chopped
½ tsp bicarbonate of soda
200g (7oz) unsalted butter
200g (7oz) light soft brown sugar
2 tbsp golden syrup
300g (10½oz) rolled oats

Method
1 Preheat the oven to 160°C (325°F/Gas 3). Line the tin with baking parchment. Place the dates and bicarbonate of soda in a pan with enough water to cover, simmer for 5 minutes, then drain, reserving the liquid. Whizz to a purée in a blender with 3 tablespoons of cooking liquid. Set aside.

2 Melt the butter, sugar, and syrup in a large pan, stirring to mix. Stir in the oats, then press half the mixture into the tin.

3 Spread the date purée over the top of the oats, then spoon the remaining oat mixture over the top. Bake for 40 minutes or until golden brown. Leave to cool in the tin for 10 minutes, then cut into 16 squares with a knife. Leave to cool completely in the tin before turning out with a fish slice.

STORE The flapjacks can be kept in an airtight container for 1 week.

BISCUITS, COOKIES, AND SLICES

Chocolate and Hazelnut Brownies

A classic American recipe, these brownies are moist and squidgy in the centre and crisp on top.

MAKES 24 · **25 MINS** · **12–15 MINS**

Special equipment
23 x 30cm (9 x 12in)
brownie tin, or similar

Ingredients
100g (3½oz) hazelnuts
175g (6oz) unsalted butter, diced
300g (10½oz) good-quality dark
  chocolate, broken into pieces
300g (10½oz) caster sugar
4 large eggs, beaten
200g (7oz) plain flour
25g (scant 1oz) cocoa powder,
  plus extra for dusting

1 Preheat the oven to 200°C (400°F/Gas 6). Scatter the hazelnuts over a baking sheet.

2 Toast the nuts in the oven for 5 minutes until browned, being careful not to burn them.

3 Remove from the oven and rub the hazelnuts in a tea towel to remove the skins.

4 Chop the hazelnuts roughly – some big chunks and some small. Set aside.

5 Line the base and sides of the tin with parchment. Some should hang over the sides.

6 Place the butter and chocolate in a heatproof bowl over a pan of simmering water.

7 Melt the butter and chocolate, stirring until smooth. Remove and leave to cool.

8 Once the mixture has cooled, mix in the sugar until very well blended.

9 Now add the eggs, a little at a time, being careful to mix well between additions.

10 Sift in the flour and cocoa powder, lifting the sieve up above the bowl to aerate.

11 Fold in the flour and cocoa until the batter is smooth and no patches of flour can be seen.

12 Stir in the chopped nuts to distribute them evenly in the batter; the batter should be thick.

13 Pour into the prepared tin and spread so the mixture fills the corners. Smooth the top.

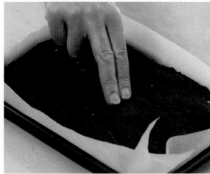

14 Bake for 12–15 minutes or until just firm to the touch on top and still soft underneath.

15 A skewer inserted should come out coated with a little batter. Remove from the oven.

16 Leave the brownie to cool completely in the tin to maintain the soft centre.

17 Lift the brownie from the tin using the edges of the parchment to get a good grip.

18 Using a long, sharp, or serrated knife, score the surface of the brownie into 24 even pieces.

19 Boil a kettle, and pour the boiling water into a shallow dish. Keep the dish close at hand.

20 Cut the brownie into 24, wiping the knife between cuts and dipping it in the hot water.

21 Sift cocoa powder over the brownies.
STORE Keep in an airtight container for 3 days.

CHOCOLATE AND HAZELNUT BROWNIES

Brownie variations

Sour Cherry and Chocolate Brownies

The sharp flavour and chewy texture of the dried sour cherries contrast wonderfully here with the rich, dark chocolate.

| MAKES 16 | 15 MINS | 20–25 MINS |

Special equipment
20 x 25cm (8 x 10in) brownie tin, or similar

Ingredients
150g (5½oz) unsalted butter, diced, plus extra for greasing
150g (5½oz) good-quality dark chocolate, broken into pieces
250g (9oz) soft light brown muscovado sugar
150g (5½oz) self-raising flour, sifted
3 eggs
1 tsp vanilla extract
100g (3½oz) dried sour cherries
100g (3½oz) dark chocolate chunks

Method
1 Preheat the oven to 180°C (350°F/Gas 4). Grease the brownie tin and line with baking parchment. Melt the butter and chocolate in a heatproof bowl over a small amount of simmering water. Remove from the heat, add the sugar, and stir well to combine thoroughly. Cool slightly.

2 Mix the eggs and vanilla extract into the chocolate mixture. Pour the wet mix into the sifted flour and fold together, being careful not to over-mix. Fold in the sour cherries and chocolate chunks.

3 Pour the brownie mixture into the tin and bake in the centre of the oven for 20–25 minutes. They are ready when the edges are firm, but the middle is soft to the touch.

4 Leave the brownie to cool in the tin for 5 minutes. Turn out and cut into squares. Put the brownies onto a wire rack to cool.

STORE The brownies will keep in an airtight container for 3 days.

BAKER'S TIP
The texture of a brownie is very much a matter of personal taste. Some people like them so squishy that they fall apart, while others prefer a firmer cake. If you like squidgy brownies, reduce the cooking time slightly.

Walnut and White Chocolate Brownies

Slightly soft in the centre, these make a tempting teatime treat.

| MAKES 16 | 10 MINS | 1 HOUR 15 MINS |

Special equipment
20cm (8in) deep square tin

Ingredients
25g (scant 1oz) unsalted butter, diced, plus extra for greasing
50g (1¾oz) good-quality dark chocolate, broken into pieces
3 eggs
1 tbsp clear honey
225g (8oz) soft light brown sugar
75g (2½oz) self-raising flour
175g (6oz) walnut pieces
25g (scant 1oz) white chocolate, chopped

Method
1 Preheat the oven to 160°C (325°F/Gas 3). Lightly grease the tin, or line the base and sides with baking parchment.

2 Put the dark chocolate and butter into a small heatproof bowl over a saucepan of simmering water until melted, stirring occasionally. Do not let the bowl touch the water. Remove the bowl from the pan and set aside to cool slightly.

3 Beat together the eggs, honey, and brown sugar, then gradually beat in the melted chocolate mixture. Sift the flour over, add the walnut pieces and white chocolate, and gently fold the ingredients together. Pour the mixture into the prepared tin.

4 Put the tin in the oven and bake for 30 minutes. Cover loosely with foil and bake for another 45 minutes. The centre should be a little soft. Leave to cool completely in the tin on a wire rack. When cold, turn out onto a board and cut into squares.

STORE The brownies will keep in an airtight container for 5 days.

White Chocolate Macadamia Blondies

A white chocolate version of the ever-popular brownie.

MAKES 24   15 MINS   20 MINS

Special equipment
20 x 25cm (8 x 10in) brownie tin, or similar

Ingredients
300g (10oz) white chocolate, broken into pieces
175g (6oz) unsalted butter, diced
300g (10oz) caster sugar
4 large eggs
225g (8oz) plain flour
100g (3½oz) macadamia nuts, roughly chopped

Method
1 Preheat the oven to 200°C (400°F/Gas 6). Line the base and sides of the tin with baking parchment. In a bowl set over a pan of simmering water, melt the chocolate and butter, stirring occasionally until smooth. Do not let the bowl touch the water. Remove and leave to cool for 20 minutes.

2 Once the chocolate has melted, mix in the sugar (the mixture may well become thick and grainy, but the eggs will loosen the mixture). Using a balloon whisk, beat in the eggs one at a time, making sure each is well mixed in before you add the next. Sift in the flour, gently fold it in, then stir in the nuts.

3 Pour the mixture into the tin and gently spread it out into the corners. Bake for 20 minutes or until just firm to the touch on top, but still soft underneath. Leave to cool completely in the tin, then cut into 24 squares, or fewer rectangles for bigger blondies.

STORE The blondies will keep in an airtight container for 5 days.

Index

Page numbers in **bold** indicate step-by-step illustrations of recipes or techniques. Page numbers in *italics* indicate Baker's Tips.

About the author

After spending years as an international model, Caroline Bretherton dedicated herself to her passion for food, founding her company, Manna Food, in 1996.

Her fresh, light, and stylish cooking soon developed a stylish following to match, with a catering clientele that included celebrities, art galleries, theatres, and fashion magazines, as well as cutting edge businesses. She later expanded the company to include an all-day eatery called Manna Café on Portobello Road, in the heart of London's Notting Hill.

A move into the media has seen her working consistently in television over the years, guesting on and presenting a wide range of food programmes for terrestrial and cable broadcasters.

More recently Caroline has worked increasingly in print, becoming a regular contributor to *The Times on Saturday*, and writing her first book *The Allotment Cookbook*.

In her spare time, Caroline tends her beloved allotment near her home in London, growing a variety of fruits, vegetables, and herbs. When she can, she indulges her passion for wild food foraging, both in the city and the country.

She is married to Luke, an academic, and has two boys, Gabriel and Isaac, who were more than happy to test the recipes for this book.

Acknowledgments

The author would like to thank
Mary-Clare, Dawn, and Alastair at Dorling Kindersley for their help and encouragement with this massive task, as well as Borra Garson and all at Deborah McKenna for all their work on my behalf. Lastly I would like to thank all my family and friends for their tremendous encouragement and appetites!

Dorling Kindersley would like to thank
The following people for their work on the photoshoot:

Art Directors
Nicky Collings, Miranda Harvey, Luis Peral, Lisa Pettibone

Props Stylist
Wei Tang

Food Stylists
Kate Blinman, Lauren Owen, Denise Smart

Home Economist Assistant
Emily Jonzen

Baking equipment used in the step-by-step photography kindly donated by Lakeland. For all your baking needs contact: www.lakeland.co.uk; or order by phone on 015394 88100.

Caroline de Souza for art direction and setting the style of the presentation stills photography.

Dorothy Kikon for editorial assistance and Anamica Roy for design assistance.

Jane Ellis for proofreading and Susan Bosanko for indexing.

Thanks to the following people for their work on the US edition:

Consultant
Kate Curnes
Americanizers
Nichole Morford and Jenny Siklós

Thanks also to Steve Crozier for retouching.